CW00344336

St George

Christopher Stace read Classics at Cambridge, then taught at Christ's Hospital and Bradfield College. He has translated a variety of classical authors: Euripides for the BBC, Plautus for Cambridge University Press, and Sophocles for performances at the Royal Exchange Theatre, Manchester (*Philoctetes* in 1982; the two *Oedipus* plays in 1987). His publications include *Florence, City of the Lily* (Dent, 1989), a celebration of his love of Italy, a translation of Jacobus de Voragine's *The Golden Legend* (Penguin, 1998), a translation of Thomas Celano's *First Life of Saint Francis of Assisi* (Triangle, 1999), and most recently *St Clare of Assisi: Her Legend and Selected Writings* (Triangle, 2001).

ST GEORGE

Patron Saint of England

Christopher Stace

TRIANGLE

Published in Great Britain in 2002 by Triangle
Society for Promoting Christian Knowledge
Holy Trinity Church
Marylebone Road
London NW1 4DU

British Library Cataloguing-in-Publication Data
A catalogue record for this book is available from the British Library

ISBN 0 281 05415 0

Typeset by Trinity Typing, Wark-on-Tweed
Printed in Great Britain by Omnia Books, Glasgow

Contents

Introduction

This is a book about England's patron saint, St George. It would be a very short book indeed if it were simply a survey of his historical life, because there is probably no saint so well known about whom so little is known. Until the sixth century, canonization was by popular acclaim, so the cult of St George is the result of interest on the part of ordinary people. What exactly was this interest, what was George's great, and seemingly immediate, appeal?

George seems as English as buttered toast and ballroom dancing, but of course he was no more English than St Patrick was Irish or St Andrew Scottish. He is an import, probably a Turk, possibly a Palestinian, possibly even a Nubian, and his name can never have been George. The balance of probabilities is that he did exist. George was one of the most celebrated and popular of the early martyrs, and he has always been specially venerated in the East. It is likely that he was a soldier. The rest is largely speculation, but the day he was martyred he stepped from history into legend.

The difficulty in writing a book on St George is not, as is generally the case with early saints, due to the scarcity of information available. Vast amounts have been written, and continue to be written, on St George. A fair-sized book could be put together on almost any one of the many subjects touched on in these chapters: on dragon-lore, for example, on persecution, on St George in folk-lore, on literary, artistic and musical references to St George, on the Knightly Orders of St George. The difficulty is what to omit.

I have devoted a sizeable number of these pages to a survey of the literary texts, because that is my chief interest, and such studies are in fact few in number. An analysis of the similarities and dissimilarities of these accounts can throw interesting light on the motives and preconceptions of the writers and the attitudes of the times in which they lived.

The written accounts of St George's life are many and various, and date generally from at least a couple of hundred years after his martyrdom. They contain hardly a single reliable detail and display a staggering diversity. If the story of his death in broad outline follows a similar pattern, the disagreement as to persons and places and chronology is utterly disconcerting. One needs to keep a very clear head. There are miracles and divine interventions. George suffers death several times and is resuscitated; he is plunged into a bath of molten lead and sawn in two; he drinks poison twice and suffers no harm.

The traditional story, known in this country long before the Norman Conquest, long before the Crusaders brought back from the Holy Land tales of the warrior saint and his miraculous powers, was endlessly told and retold, all the time gathering new details and fresh elaborations. And in time George found himself in Libya slaying a dragon and making thousands of converts to the faith. His story grew wings. Yet, if we disbelieve its details, we can still trust in the substance of the story. We shall see that George is a hydra-like figure with many different heads. He has developed from a historical martyr into a symbol rooted deeply in our national consciousness. Tradition is of the utmost importance to civilization: in maintaining traditions we in the present link ourselves with all past generations and those to come.

We start with the most famous version of the legend, that given in Jacobus de Voragine's *The Golden Legend* (thirteenth century), which presents us with the first written account of the fight with the dragon. This is followed by a review of the earliest Greek and Latin Lives and a brief look at the more elaborate oriental legends, versions of the story that appeared in Coptic, Ethiopic, Arabic and Syriac a few centuries after George's martyrdom.

Chapter 3 deals with St George's importance in the Crusades, follows his translation from the Near East to England, and includes a survey of the first Anglo-Saxon Life of St George, by Aelfric (*c.*993–8).

The celebrated dragon does not make his appearance until Chapter 4. The dragon episode was added late, and is of uncertain relationship to the passion of St George. This chapter looks at dragons and dragon-combats in general, and attempts to make sense of St George's unlikely involvement with the Libyan dragon of Silene.

The penultimate chapter is concerned with the place of St George in medieval English life at the height of his popularity, the effect of the Reformation on his cult, and his varying fortunes during the reigns of post-Reformation monarchs. We shall look at some of the visual evidence for his legend – the sculptures, the stained-glass windows and wall paintings that survive.

A final section will attempt to cover the survival and development of the cult of St George in the modern era, and to draw together the many strands of the narrative.

A short survey can never hope to be exhaustive; but what follows, together with some of the other works listed in the Bibliography, may at least serve to encourage readers to pursue their own researches, to reassess for themselves the hero who is their national figure-head – the knight in shining white armour, the *chevalier sans peur et sans reproche* who has typified our country's aspirations and still symbolizes our nation's history.

Select Bibliography

Bengston, J., 'St George and the Formation of English Nationalism', in *Journal of Medieval and Early Modern Studies* 27, Spring 1997, pp. 317–40.

Budge, Sir E. A. Wallis, *George of Lydda, The Patron Saint of England: A Study of the Cultus of St George in Ethiopia*, London, Luzac and Co., 1930. Indispensable for the eastern versions.

Bulley, Margaret, *St George for Merrie England*, London, George Allen, 1908.

Chambers, E. K., *The Mediaeval Stage*, Oxford, OUP, 1903.

Delehaye, H., SJ, *The Legends of the Saints: An Introduction to Hagiography* (English translation V. M. Crawford), London, Longman, Green and Co., 1907.

Delehaye, H., SJ, *Les légendes grecques des saints militaires*, Paris, Librairie Alphonse Picard, 1909.

Duffy, Eamon, *The Stripping of the Altars: Traditional Religion in England 1400–1580*, New Haven, Yale University Press, 1992.

Elder, Isabel H., *George of Lydda*, London, Covenant Publishing, 1949.

Fox, Sir David Scott, *Saint George: The Saint with Three Faces*, London, Kensal Press, 1983. Extremely readable and wide-ranging.

Heer, Friedrich, *The Medieval World: Europe 1100–1350*, translated by Janet Sondheimer, London, Weidenfeld, 1962.

Howell, David, 'Saint George as Intercessor', in *Byzantion* xxxix, 1969, pp. 121–36.

Krumbacher, K., *Der heilige Georg in der griechischen Überlieferung*, Munich, Abhandlungen der Königlich Bayerischen Akademie, 1911. Magisterial edition of the Greek manuscript tradition.

Le Goff, Jacques (ed.), *L'Uomo Medievale*, Roma-Bari, 1987; translated by Lydia G. Cochrane, *The Medieval World*, London, Parkgate Books, 1990.

McClendon, Muriel C., 'A Moveable Feast: Saint George's Day Celebrations and Religious Change in Early Modern England', in *Journal of British Studies* 38, January 1999, number 1, pp. 1–27.

Mâle, E., *L'Art Religieux du XIIIe siècle en France*, Paris, 1898; translated by Dora Nussey, *The Gothic Image: Religious Art in France of the Thirteenth Century*, US, Harper Torchbook, 1958.

Marcus, G. J., *St George of England*, London, Williams and Norgate, 1929.

Riches, Samantha, *St George: Hero, Martyr and Myth*, Stroud, Sutton Publishing, 2000. Indispensable update. Concentrates primarily on period 1300–1550 and visual references to the legend. Richly illustrated.

Thurston, Fr Herbert, 'St George', in *The Month* 74, April 1892, pp. 457–83.

Tiddy, R. J. E., *The Mummers' Play*, Chicheley, 1972.

Voragine, Jacobus de, *The Golden Legend*, translated by Christopher Stace with an introduction by Richard Hamer, Harmondsworth, Penguin, 1998.

Weinstein, Donald, and Bell, Rudolph M., *Saints and Society*, Chicago, University of Chicago Press, 1982.

Acknowledgements

Many people have helped me in the preparation of this volume and I offer grateful thanks to the following:

David Jones and Steve Herbert for bibliographical services;
Richard Hamer for help with Early English texts and matters hagiographical;
Dr Samantha Riches for her book, for patiently answering my questions, and for supplying me with some rare material;
Revd Denis Mulliner for help with the Anglican Calendar;
John Wesley Harding and Barry Dransfield for books on ballads and mummers' plays;
and Freda Crockford for reading the typescript and improving it in many ways.

Finally a word of thanks to the British Library; to Cambridge University Library; to the harassed but unfailingly helpful staff of Hastings Library; and to the friendly librarian and library of the Franciscan International Study Centre, Canterbury, where I have always been made welcome.

Chronological Table of Events

249–51	Reign of Decius
253–60	Reign of Valerian
284–305	Reign of Diocletian
308–37	Reign of Constantine the Great
325	Council of Nicaea
494	Decree of Pope Gelasius
4th/5th c	Nubian Life of St George
5th c	Vienna Palimpsest (Greek)
5th/6th c	Early Latin and oriental Lives of St George
c.1000	Aelfric's *Life of St George*
1061	Church at Doncaster dedicated to St George
1080–1120	Lewes Group of wall paintings executed
1095	First Crusade proclaimed
c.1100	Murals painted at e.g. Hardham, Sussex
1191–2	Richard I discovers George's tomb at Lydda (?)
1222	Synod of Oxford: 23 April a holiday (second class)
1265	Jacobus de Voragine's *The Golden Legend*
1327–77	**Reign of Edward III**
1348	Order of the Garter instituted
14th c (mid)	Red cross banner adopted as arms of City of London
1399	St George's Day a national holiday
c.1400	Mirk's *Festial*
1413–22	**Reign of Henry V**
c.1425	Lydgate's *Life*
1438	*Gilte Legende*
1415	Agincourt; 23 April becomes a *festum duplex*
1483	Caxton's *Golden Legend*
1505	*Georgius* of the Mantuan

1509–47	**Reign of Henry VIII**
1536	Most religious holidays abrogated, but 23 April retained
1547–53	**Reign of Edward VI**
1547	Chantries Act. Edward bans all processions
1549	First Book of Common Prayer: 23 April a red-letter day
1552	Revised Book of Common Prayer: 23 April a black-letter day and St George's Day moved to 21 April
1553–8	**Reign of Mary**
1558–1603	**Reign of Elizabeth I**
1560	23 April again a national holiday
1597	Johnson's *The Seven Champions of Christendom*
1960	23 April removed from Roman Calendar
1969	23 April becomes optional commemoration
1980	No propers for 23 April in ASB
1997	23 April restored as major feast in Anglican Calendar

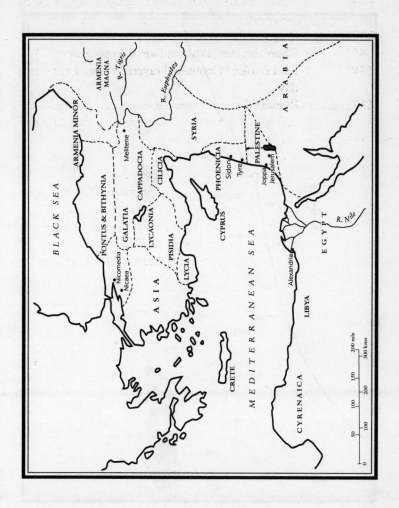

Map 1: Eastern Mediterranean and Near East *c.*300 AD

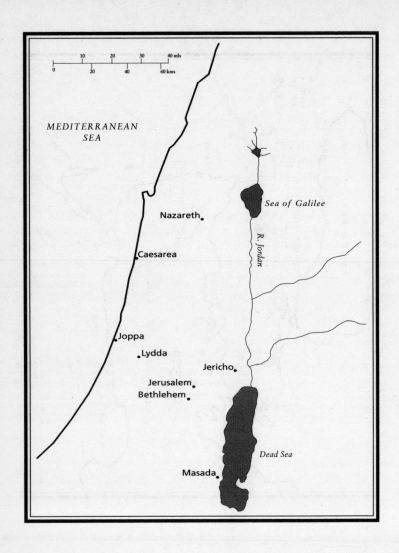

Map 2: Palestine in the Early Christian Era

1

THE GOLDEN LEGEND

It is the year of our Lord 1350, the twenty-third year of the reign of Edward III. We are in the Benedictine Abbey of St George at Thetford, Norfolk. The rigours of Lent and the joys of Easter are some weeks past. Springtide in England: in the Abbey gardens catkins dust the hedgerows and the brothers are busy digging and planting. Just after noon a small bell rings and gratefully they straighten their backs and file in a silent line towards the refectory, where they take their accustomed places at the long heavy table. Wine today, perhaps even fowl. But for some days now the brothers have been anticipating the occasion. Already Vigils, in the small hours of the night, has announced the fact, and Lauds and Prime have left them in no doubt: it is nine days before the kalends of May, 23 April – the feast day of their patron St George.

The Abbot sings grace, the brothers are seated, and the appointed brother lector begins, his voice quavering at first, then steadying as he proceeds.

'In the name of the Father, the Son and the Holy Ghost': a reading from *The Golden Legend* of Jacobus de Voragine:

The name George comes from *geos*, meaning earth, and *orge*, meaning to till, so 'one who tills the earth', that is his own flesh. Now Augustine in his book *On the Trinity* says that good earth is to be found on the tops of mountains, in the temperate climate of the hills, and on the level of the plains. The first is good for lush grass, the second for vines, the third for wheat and grain. Thus the blessed George

1

raised himself on high through despising lowly things and so produced the verdure of purity; he was temperate by virtue of his discernment, and so produced the wine of inward gladness; and lowly because of his humility, and so produced the fruits of good works.

Or George could be derived from *gerar*, holy, and *gyon*, sand, so meaning 'holy sand'. For he was like sand, heavy with the weight of his virtues, yet small through his humility, and dry of the lusts of the flesh.

Or George could come from *gerar*, holy, and *gyon*, wrestling: he was a 'holy wrestler' because he wrestled with the dragon and his executioner.

Or the name comes from *gero*, a pilgrim, and *gir*, 'cut off', and *ys*, counsellor: for he was a pilgrim in his disdain for the world, 'cut off' when he won his crown of martyrdom, and a counsellor in his preaching of the kingdom.

At the Council of Nicaea his legend was numbered among the apocryphal writings because there is no authentic account of his martyrdom. In Bede's Calendar we read that he suffered in the Persian city of Diospolis, which was formerly called Lydda, and is near Joppa. Elsewhere it is said that he suffered under the Emperors Diocletian and Maximian; other authors state that it was under the Persian emperor Dacian,[1] in the presence of 70 of his subject kings. Others say he was martyred under the prefect Dacian, in the reign of Diocletian and Maximian.

George was a native of Cappadocia and a tribune in the Roman army. One day he came to Silena, a city in the province of Libya. Close by this city was a vast lake, as big as an inland sea, where a pestilential dragon had its lair. The people had often risen in arms against it, but the dragon always put them to flight, and would venture right up to the city walls and asphyxiate everyone with its noxious breath. So the citizens were compelled to feed it two sheep every day in order to allay its fury, otherwise it would make straight for the city walls and poison the air, causing a great many deaths. But in time, since their flocks were not large, the supply of sheep began to run out, and the citizens decided to give the dragon one sheep and one human being. The names of the victims were drawn by lot, and no-one of either sex was excluded. But in due course nearly all the young folk were eaten up, and one day the lot fell upon the only daughter of the king, and the people seized her to feed her to the dragon. The king was heartbroken. 'Take my gold and silver,' he cried. 'Take half my realm, and let my daughter go, save her from this dreadful death.' But the people rounded on him in fury. 'It was you who issued this decree, your majesty, and, now all our children are dead, you want to save your own daughter? If you do not sacrifice your daughter and do what you forced all the rest of us to do, we will burn you alive, you and all your household.' At this the king began to weep for his daughter. 'Woe is me!' he cried. 'My sweetest child, what am I to do about you? What can I say? Can I no more hope to see your wedding day?' Turning to the people, he said: 'I beg you, grant me a week's grace in which to mourn my daughter.' To this the people agreed, but at the end of the week they came back and demanded angrily: 'How can you destroy your subjects just for your daughter's sake? We are all dying from the breath of the dragon!' Then the king, seeing that he could not save his daughter, dressed her in all her regal finery and embracing her, said tearfully: 'Alas, my sweetest daughter, I thought to see you rear royal children at your bosom, and now you are going to be devoured by the dragon! Alas, my sweetest child, I hoped to invite all the nobility to your wedding, to deck the palace with pearls, to hear the music of timbrels and trumpets, and now you are going to be devoured by the dragon!' He kissed her and let her go with a final word. 'Oh, my daughter, would I had died before you, rather than lose you in this way!' She then fell at her father's feet, asking his blessing, and, when in a flood of tears he had blessed her, she set off towards the lake.

3

Now St George happened to be passing that way, and when he saw her weeping, he asked her what was the matter. 'Good youth,' she replied, 'mount your horse with all speed and flee, or you will share my fate and die as I must.' 'Do not be afraid, my child,' George told her. 'But tell me, what are you waiting here for, and why are all these people watching?' 'Good youth,' she replied, 'I see you have a noble heart, but do you want to die with me? Make haste and flee!' George told her: 'I shall not move from here until you tell me what is the matter.' So then she told him the whole story, and George said: 'My child, do not be afraid, for in the name of Christ I will help you.' 'You are a brave knight,' she replied. 'But do not perish with me. It is enough that I die, for you cannot save me, you would only die with me.' While they were talking the dragon suddenly lifted its head from the lake. Trembling, the young girl cried: 'Flee, good lord, make haste and flee!' But George mounted his horse, armed himself with the sign of the cross, and bravely went to meet the dragon as it came towards him. Brandishing his lance and commending himself to God, he dealt the beast such a deadly wound that he threw it to the ground. He called to the princess: 'Throw your girdle round the dragon's neck. Do not be afraid, child.' She did as he told her, and the dragon followed her as meekly as a puppy. She led it into the city, but when the people saw it they began to run for the mountains and hills, crying: 'Help! We are all done for!' But St George waved at them to come back. 'Do not be afraid,' he told them. 'The Lord has sent me to free you from the tyranny of the dragon. Only believe in Christ and be baptized, every one of you, and I will slay your dragon.'

So the king and all the people were baptized and St George drew his sword and slew the dragon, and gave orders that it should be carried outside the city walls. Four pairs of oxen dragged the beast out of the city and left it on a broad open plain. That day twenty thousand were baptized,

4

not counting women and children. The king built a large and splendid church there in honour of Blessed Mary and St George, and from its altar there still issues a natural spring whose waters cure all illnesses. The king also offered St George a large sum of money, but the saint refused to accept it, and ordered it to be given to the poor. He then gave the king four brief rules of life: to cherish the Church of God; to honour priests; to be scrupulous in attending mass, and always to be mindful of the poor. With that he kissed the king farewell and left. We read in some sources, however, that when the dragon was rushing towards the girl to devour her, George actually armed himself with a cross, then attacked and killed the dragon.

At this time, during the principate of Diocletian and Maximian, the prefect Dacian started such a vicious persecution of the Christians that within a single month seventeen thousand won the crown of martyrdom, and, as a result, threatened as they were with torture of every kind, many Christians gave in and offered sacrifice to the idols. When he saw this, St George was grief-stricken; he gave away all his possessions, laid aside his soldier's uniform and dressed as a Christian. Then he ran out into the midst of the crowds and cried: 'All the gods of the heathen are demons! It was our Lord who made the heavens!' The prefect angrily rejoined: 'How dare you presume to call our gods demons! Tell me, where do you come from, and what is your name?' George answered him: 'My name is George, and I come from a noble family of Cappadocia. With Christ's help I have conquered Palestine;[2] but now I have left everything in order to be more free to serve the God of heaven.' The prefect saw that he could not sway him, and ordered him to be put to the rack and torn limb from limb with iron hooks. Brands were thrust against his sides to sear his flesh, and where his entrails showed through, the prefect had salt rubbed in the wounds. But that same night the Lord appeared to George in a great blaze of light and tenderly comforted him: so blissful was this vision and so sweet the words he spoke that George thought nothing of his pain.

Dacian saw he could not conquer his prisoner by torture, so he summoned a sorcerer and told him: 'The Christians are laughing at our tortures. They must be using some magic of theirs. They show utter disrespect for the worship of our gods.' The sorcerer replied: 'If I cannot overcome this magic, then you can have my head!' He then worked his sorcery, called on the names of his gods, mixed some poison in some wine and gave it to blessed George to drink. But the saint made the sign of the cross over the cup and drained it without suffering the slightest harm. So the sorcerer mixed a stronger poison with the wine, but again, after making the sign of the cross, George drank it without coming to any harm. When he saw this, the sorcerer fell at once at the saint's feet, tearfully begged his pardon, and asked to become a Christian. Soon after, in fact, the prefect had him beheaded for this. The following day Dacian had George tied on a wheel fitted all round with sharp, two-edged swords, but the wheel instantly fell apart, and George was found to be quite unhurt. In a rage the prefect ordered him to be plunged into a cauldron of molten lead, but George made the sign of the cross, got in, and with God's help found it no hotter than a refreshing bath.

Seeing that he could break George through neither threats nor tortures, Dacian now thought to win him over by persuasion. 'George, my son,' he said, 'you can see how indulgent our gods are. They put up with your blasphemy so patiently, and still they are ready to forgive you, if you will turn to them. So come, my dearest son, do as I advise you: abandon your superstition and sacrifice to our gods, and win great honours from them and from ourselves, too.' With a smile George replied: 'Why did you not use persuasion in the first place, rather than trying to break me with tortures? Very well, I am prepared to do what you want.' Dacian, fooled by George's assurance, was delighted: he

6

had the herald call the whole people together to see George, who had resisted so long, finally give in and offer sacrifice. The whole city was decked out as for a festival, and there was general rejoicing as George entered the temple to offer sacrifice, and all the people stood by in happy anticipation. But instead of sacrificing, George knelt and prayed for the Lord to destroy the temple and all its idols, destroy it so completely that, for the glory of God and the conversion of the people, absolutely nothing was left of it. At once fire fell from heaven and burnt the temple, its idols and priests, to a cinder, and the earth gaped open and swallowed up the remains . . .

When Dacian learnt what George had done, he had him brought before him. 'You evil man!' he cried. 'What sorcery of yours is this? How could you commit so heinous a crime?' George replied: 'It is not as you think, my lord. Come along with me and see me sacrifice again.' Dacian retorted: 'I know what you are up to. You want the earth to swallow me, too, as you made it swallow the temple of my gods.' 'Poor wretch,' George said. 'Tell me, how can your gods help you, when they could not help themselves?' The prefect now flew into a mad rage. 'I am finished! I shall die!' he told his wife Alexandria. 'I cannot bear to see this man get the better of me!' 'Cruel, murderous tyrant!' she replied. 'Did I not often tell you to stop persecuting the Christians because their God was fighting on their side? And now let me tell you this: I myself wish to become a Christian.' Dumbfounded, the prefect cried: 'No! This is too much to bear! Have you, too, been seduced by them?' So he had her hung up by her hair and cruelly beaten with scourges. While she was being beaten, she said to George: 'George, hero of the true faith, what do you think will become of me? I have not yet been reborn in the waters of baptism.' George answered: 'Do not be afraid, my daughter. The blood you shed will be your baptism and your crown.' Then, with a prayer on her lips, Alexandria breathed her last . . .

7

The following day George was condemned to be dragged through the length and breadth of the city and then beheaded. He prayed to the Lord that whoever implored his aid might have his prayer granted, and a heavenly voice came to him, saying that his wish would be fulfilled. When he had finished praying, he was beheaded, and thus he accomplished this martyrdom in the reign of Diocletian and Maximian, which began around the year of our Lord 287. As for Dacian, when he was returning to the palace from the place of execution, fire fell from heaven and consumed him and all his attendants with him . . .

The brothers have now finished their meal and, rising with the Abbot to give thanks, they make their way back to their work.

And that (with one or two tiny omissions) is the story of George and the dragon, or that story in its developed medieval form as told by the Blessed Jacobus de Voragine, a Dominican monk who became Archbishop of Genoa, and between 1259 and 1265 compiled *The Golden Legend*, a collection of lives of the saints celebrated within the liturgical calendar of his day, together with short accounts of the main feasts of the Christian year. Originally intended as a lectionary for Dominican houses, its popularity rapidly spread; it was to be hugely successful, one of the most widely read books of medieval times, and by the end of the Middle Ages it had appeared in translation in most European languages. Almost from its first publication it exercised an enormous influence in England, and when Caxton printed his version of the *Legend* in 1483 it became the standard collection of hagiographies. It was his most popular production and went into several reprints.

And did his readers believe such tales? Did they truly believe in dragons and invincible knights in shining armour? Certainly there was in medieval times a marked difference in the outlook of Christians. 'God and the Evil One, the blessed saints and the wicked demons,' one scholar has written, 'were just as close and familiar as the animals and the implements which made up the routine of daily life.'[3]

Life was fragile, the natural world was full of terrors: there were plagues and famines and feuds and sudden inexplicable deaths. In such times men's faith embraced a God who was not only a God of joy but a God of terror and death. (How many of our churches had 'Dooms' in the arch over the crossing, an ever-present reminder of death and judgement? Only look at the Omnipotent as he sits in majesty there, still inexorably stern in the faded mural! Then let your gaze sink to the gibbets and the torment of the souls in hell beneath.) Evil was omnipresent, life a continual battle between evil spirits and the army of Christ. Among the people, mass was regarded as a battle with the devil: the priest, clothed in the vestments of salvation, was their leader in this struggle, and would lead them into their heavenly home. Mass was a tribunal, where a stern God sat as judge, the devil prosecuted, and the priest defended them.[4] One could survive the ghastliness of life only by constantly warring for right and by living the Christian life, by going to church, observing the ceremonies of the Christian year, by fasting and giving alms. The church alone, with its stout, cool walls, provided a sanctuary where evil spirits or hobgoblins dared not enter. On its walls were the statues and frescoes which graphically portrayed the stories folk heard from the preachers: the martyrs, flayed, racked, boiled alive – every conceivable physical agony was depicted in loving detail to horrify the faithful and to enlist their sympathy for the heroic victim. Here is Cecilia with her throat slit; Agatha minus her breasts; Lucia with her eyes on a plate; the toothless Apollonia; Laurence roasted alive; John the Evangelist boiled in oil; Sebastian bristling with arrows. One must remember, too, that illiteracy was widespread: visual images and the tales told by preachers were all that a large number knew of the saints and the stories of the Bible. And when darkness fell, the grim judgement scenes, the beasts and demons, the agonized saints, the shrieks of the damned and the glee of their tormentors so familiar from glass window, reredos and capital and ceiling must have seemed horribly real.

God, all-powerful, could and did work wonders through his holy ones. He could revive the dead and make his saints invincible: what could he not do?

9

Demons? Everyone knew what demons looked like. They were painted in attitudes and in colours that burnt themselves into the subconscious medieval mind. They could be dog-like and winged like pterodactyls, with ramshorns and staring ribs, goatee beards, bristled and scaled, with talons and curly tails, pointing Gothic ears and gappy crocodile teeth, or with upward curving tusks at the edge of their mouths, werewolf-like or dragon-like, half-human mutations, horned with jagged dinosaur spines and piggy eyes. They could be large enough to stand on their hind legs and wrestle with monks, or tiny enough to zoom through the air in malevolent clusters. You can see them in Spinello Aretino's fresco cycle of St Benedict in San Miniato, Florence. Or go to the Spanish chapel there and look at Andrea da Firenze's frescoes of the descent of Christ into Limbo; or lie on a dark night on the pavement of the Baptistry and wait until dawn lights up the ceiling.

And dragons were a commonplace. We shall have much to say about dragons in a later chapter. But we are leaping ahead, and by hundreds of years. We must return to the historical George, and for a while forget the dragon.

NOTES

1 Text uncertain. Some manuscripts have 'Diocletian' here.
2 Meaning uncertain. Caxton's version omits the reference to Palestine.
3 Friedrich Heer, *The Medieval World*, p. 38.
4 Heer, *The Medieval World*, p. 36.

2

SOURCES: THE FACTS AND THE ACTS

If very little is known of George's life, his existence is nowadays generally accepted. The arguments are mostly circumstantial, but they are strong arguments. Beneath all the divergent traditions about him there seems to be a bedrock of historical fact. Nothing else could satisfactorily explain the existence of his cult, which was both early and widespread, or the early dedication of churches to him. Such evidence as there is seems to support the tradition that he was martyred at or near Lydda in Palestine (on the plain of Sharon, some 12 miles from Jaffa (Joppa), and 24 miles from Jerusalem) either late in the third century or early in the fourth century AD.[1] Lydda was certainly the centre of his cult and veneration from earliest times, and such references as we have from early pilgrims (sixth–eighth centuries) all confirm Lydda as his resting place. He is said to have served in the Roman army. A cultus which goes back to very early times and has always been centred on one definite locality is a cogent historical argument.

According to the Acta (the accounts of his life composed for public reading in churches and intended for the edification and instruction of both lay and clergy), and information given us by St Simeon Metaphrastes (tenth century) quoting the writings of St Andrew of Crete (c.660–740), George was from Cappadocia in central Turkey, became a tribune (senior officer) in the Roman army and was beheaded for confessing the Christian faith during a time of persecution. Like many others he refused to sacrifice to the Roman gods, and was tortured and executed. All the sources stress the heroic endurance of St George during his passion, and there is a general consensus that he came from Cappadocia, held the rank of tribune, and was beheaded under Diocletian (284–305). Some state that his corpse was transported from Nicomedia to his mother's family estate in Lydda. But the circumstances surrounding his passion and death must have been unusual or his fame would hardly have been so immediate or lasted so long.

Such are the bare bones of the story. Very soon they were to be fleshed out with a mass of hagiographical material, much of which clearly came from the lives of other martyrs.

Eusebius of Caesarea, writing c.322, speaks of 'a man of the greatest distinction' who was put to death by the Emperor Diocletian at Nicomedia (an imperial residence in Bithynia, in north-east modern Turkey) on 23 April 303, but he gives no details of his name or his country.[2] He may just possibly be referring to George. Thousands upon thousands were martyred in Diocletian's persecution, which began in 303 and continued with varying degrees of intensity throughout the Empire until 311. But (to reiterate) there must have been something extraordinary about George's suffering and death, because he rapidly became celebrated as a great saint in Palestine, where he was venerated together with Moses and Elijah and Michael, and his cult spread rapidly through Christendom. Churches and monasteries were soon dedicated to him throughout the Near East. George was known as a great warrior martyr (he was associated with, and sometimes confused with, Sts Demetrius and Maurice), a man of superhuman bravery, a champion of Christ, a defender of the defenceless. He was the knight on a white charger who rode to the rescue of all who called on him, especially the Christian communities who were constantly troubled by Saracens.

The oldest extant martyrology, a fifth-century Syriac manuscript in the British Museum, though compiled in the country where George is held in highest veneration, says nothing of our saint under 23 April. But under 24 April there is an agonizing lacuna in the crucial place: we are told of 'Anthimus . . . and five other conquerors'. And the tenth-century Byzantine Georgius Cedrenus, in his history of the Diocletian persecution, among the casualties lists: 'Peter Bishop of Alexandria, Anthimus of Nicomedia, and Procopius and George, the illustrious martyrs'.

The so-called *Martyrology of St Jerome*, an eighth- or ninth-century document, mentions the name of George under 23 April, but without special emphasis, and with no details as to the date or place of his martyrdom, though under 24 and 25 April it includes references to St George, on the 24th stating that in some places this day was kept as his feast day.

The earliest undeniable reference to our saint came in the decree of Pope Gelasius passed in Rome in 494 AD,[3] which condemns the Acta of certain martyrs as ridiculous and the work of ignorant people. Gelasius ordered the suppression of such Acta as those of Sts Cyriacus and Julitta, and the passion of George. He included George among those saints 'whose names are justly reverenced among men, but whose actions are known only to God'. It need hardly be said that he was attacking the extravagant accretions to the story, not the basic account of George's martyrdom. The same goes for the Reformation scholars and divines who heaped scorn on St George. Many centuries later Edward Gibbon (author of *Decline and Fall*) mischievously identified him with *another* George of Cappadocia, a heretical Archbishop of Alexandria, who was murdered by the rabble on Christmas Eve in 361. (But some features of this George's martyrdom do seem to have become parts of St George's story, and indeed this confusion may be the origin of the tradition that St George came from Cappadocia.) This identification was finally conclusively disproved when in the nineteenth century two ancient churches of St George were discovered in Syria. Their exact dating is problematical, but it seems that they were dedicated to the saint within 50 years of his death. The church of St George at Thessalonika, too, is thought by some to date back to the fourth century.

In Christian literature, whether eastern or western, evidence for devotion to St George is relatively late. Apart from the mention by the sixth-century historian Procopius of the building of a church to St George in Armenia by the Emperor Justinian, there is nothing to testify to the official recognition of his cultus until Pope Zacharias (741–52) discovered the martyr's head in a reliquary during his rebuilding of the Lateran Palace (a Greek inscription conveniently identifying the contents), and had the precious relic taken, accompanied by hymns and canticles, to the church of San Giorgio in Velabro, where it proceeded to work prodigious miracles. But George was venerated in Rome by the fifth century; and when in 610 the Pantheon was converted into a church, one of the reliquaries installed was of St George. The Life of St Theodore of Sykeon (c.540–613) vividly attests the veneration of St George in the East: St Theodore himself was devoted to the saint, and visited by him in visions. The Greeks called George *megalomartyr*, 'the great martyr', and *tropaiophoros*, 'the victory bearer'. In France, Clovis (c.466–511), founder of the Merovingian dynasty, dedicated a monastery to the saint at Baralle in 512. Probably St George first became well known in England through Adamnan of Iona (625–704), who wrote about the pilgrimage to the Holy Land of a Gallic bishop named Arculf. His fame reached Ireland, too: Oengus's *Félire* (a martyrology finished early in the ninth century) calls St George 'a sun of victories'.

The Acts of St George were originally composed in Greek, which would have been understood in the monasteries of Syria and Egypt, and could presumably have been translated into the Syrian dialect of Palestine for his family and fellow townspeople. From this all the other accounts were ultimately derived. These Acts, translated subsequently into Latin, Syriac, Coptic, Ethiopic, Arabic and Armenian, deal with George's passion (suffering) and martyrdom, sometimes with bewildering inconsistencies as to names and places and dating. In the interests of clarity, therefore, it is best to simplify.

The earliest known narrative is a large fragment written in Greek which was discovered at Qasr Ibrîm in 1964 during excavations preceding the construction of the Aswan Dam. According to this fragment, dated 350–500 AD, George, though the son of a Cappadocian, lived in Nobatia, northern Nubia. (Interestingly this same area, the Nile River valley, was the home

14

of those other celebrated warrior saints Demetrius, Mercurius and Theodore, all of whom died in the persecutions of Decian (250) and Diocletian.) He was born in the reign of Aurelian (270–5 AD). His mother, Polychronia ('Aged'), a Christian, has him secretly baptized without the knowledge of her husband Gerontius ('Old Man'). George advances rapidly in the imperial service and travels to the king's court at Diospolis (Lydda) to apply for promotion to the rank of *comes*. There he is horrified by the worship of Apollo and Heracles and hears of a decree sentencing Christians to death. Bravely he confronts the authorities and denounces their idolatry. He suffers a variety of fiendish tortures, but is healed miraculously and freed from gaol by the Archangel Michael. Many people are converted, including the queen herself. When George desecrates the temples of the heathen gods he is taken before the king and beheaded, along with the queen and many thousands of others.

This, the earliest version of the life of the saint, proceeds along lines that will become familiar. But the document's early date is no proof of its authenticity. Certainly the chronology does not agree with the generally accepted framework of events, and other details of the story are clearly unhistorical.

The Nubian version apart, the earliest important Life of St George is found in a fragmentary fifth-century Greek palimpsest (a manuscript in which the original text has been erased and written over) in Vienna, and it is full of fancies. There are five fragments: (1) Satan stirs up King Dadianos (Dacian) of Persia to persecute the Christians; (2) George is told by God that he will be persecuted for seven years by 70 kings, he will be four times killed, and thrice revived by the Almighty; (3) he is given poison by a magician, who, to demonstrate his powers, splits a bull in two with one of his spells; (4) George asks time for a final prayer before his execution; (5) God assures him that he will hear anyone in need who invokes the name of George. The fragments are short, but there is enough to show that it is based on the same Greek original as the oldest Latin Lives and also the oriental Lives, especially the Coptic version.

In a later, complete Greek version of the same tradition[4] we are told that George was a Cappadocian, but has lived in Palestine. At the age of 22, having distinguished himself in the imperial army, he goes to the court of Dacian ('Dadianos'), 'an abysmal dragon', to ask for confirmation as *eparchos* ('military commander' or 'governor'). Dacian has announced a persecution of Christians, and amassed a vast array of implements of torture to terrify them: anyone who will not sacrifice to his gods will die. Shocked by the idolatry he sees, George distributes his goods and gives his money to the poor. He is interrogated and invited to sacrifice to the idols, but he refuses, and argues his case vigorously. He is variously tortured. The magician Athanasius tries to poison him but fails, is converted to the faith, and put to death. Next George is cut into ten pieces on a wheel, but the Archangel Michael blows his trumpet, the Lord heals him, and George appears again before the kings, who cannot believe their eyes. The general Anatolius is converted by this miracle, with his whole army, amounting to 3,099 souls (plus one woman). They are all summarily executed. George has molten lead poured down his throat and 60 nails driven into his skull. In prison, he is visited by the Lord who tells him that his passion will last seven years, he will die three times and be revived, but the fourth time he will win his crown of glory.

King Magnentius promises to be converted if George causes some wooden thrones to bear fruit, but when George does this he ascribes the miracle to his own gods. George is sawn in two and dies; his body is rendered down in a cauldron of lead, pitch and tallow, and buried. But the Archangel Gabriel gathers up his remains and the Lord revives him.

George returns to the palace where a woman named Scholastike asks him to revive her son's dead ox. He obliges her. Now King 'Trakylinos' (Tranquillinus) asks George to bring to life some dead souls: he does so, and five men, nine women and three children, 400 years dead, rise from a sarcophagus. When they ask for baptism, George stamps on the ground, a spring wells up, and he baptizes them.

Dacian is astounded, and in order to compromise George sends him to the house of a poor widow. She is too poor to offer him food, but bread is miraculously provided by the Archangel Michael. A house beam sprouts roots and leaves and grows to a great height. George also restores the sight of her deaf, blind and lame son.

George suffers more fiendish torments: he dies and is thrown onto a hilltop to be devoured by birds of prey. Amid thunder and lightning he is revived a third time, and the soldiers who cast his body out are at once converted and baptized.

The king now attempts to win George over by persuasion. George pretends to yield (this motif seems invariable in the Lives), and is taken to meet Queen Alexandra in the palace. She is converted. When the poor widow hears that her hero George is to sacrifice to the idols she cries out in dismay. But George merely laughs. He cures her son of his lameness and deafness and enlists his aid. Instead of sacrificing to them, George destroys the idols of the temple.

When Alexandra confesses her new allegiance, the king's rage is terrible; she is tortured cruelly and executed. George too is sentenced to death. His mother Polychronia argues with the king and is tortured and put to death. Before he is beheaded George prays for fire to fall from heaven and consume Dacian and his associates.

In another Greek version[5] the passion takes place during the reign of Diocletian, and it is his right-hand-man, the prefect Magnentius, who interrogates George. Two generals of the imperial army, Anatolius and Protoleos, are converted (and executed). At Magnentius' behest George revives a dead man, and resuscitates the dead ox of a farmer called Glycerius, who is subsequently converted (and of course executed). Alexandra, the empress, is converted, begs to share George's fate, but in fact dies peacefully before George is beheaded.

This last account (like other early manuscripts, including probably the Vienna Palimpsest) closes with a declaration of authenticity by 'Pasicrates, servant of George'. Delehaye has demonstrated that this is a common device used by the hagiographer to add verisimilitude to events he has either invented or drawn from some unspecified written document.[6] Note also the disappearance of Dacian ('Dadianos') and the dating of the passion during the reign of the Roman emperor Diocletian (284–305). It is true that George is generally thought to have been martyred under this emperor, but the first time Diocletian is reliably mentioned in connection with the martyr is in a work attributed to St Andrew of Crete (*c*.660–740), and the precise dating may be no more than an attempt to lend the legend some historical 'authenticity'. In hagiography the name Diocletian became simply a synonym for 'executioner', the personification of an abstraction.

The oldest Latin versions are contained in the *Codex Gallicanus* and *Codex Sangallensis*, whose texts on internal evidence appear to have been composed even before the Vulgate was generally in circulation. These two manuscripts (translations from the Greek), are independent and verbally quite different from each other. From them are derived all the versions in the languages of western Europe. As the story develops, rather like a game of Chinese Whispers, we see a tension between 'the credulous love of the marvellous which existed in more vulgar souls',[7] and (among more critical minds) a tendency to rationalize and correct, to cut down extravagant fancies and to set the narrative in a recognizable historical framework. Such other Latin versions as exist represent the earlier or later stages in this process.

In the ninth-century *Codex Gallicanus* the story proceeds along the now familiar lines: George is a holy man of God, a Cappadocian with many soldiers under his command. He confronts the cruel Dacian, king of the Persians, who with 72 client kings is persecuting the Christians. Despite suffering terrible tortures (among which his head is clubbed until his brains issue through his nostrils) he survives miraculously. A sorcerer splits a bull in two and joins it together again; but George drinks his potions unharmed. George is torn into pieces on a wheel and dies; his bones are thrown into a well; but the Lord, amid thunder and earth tremors, reassembles him. At this a military commander is converted, with all his army. There are more hideous tortures. George performs a miracle, making chairs sprout leaves, but is sawn in two for his pains and boiled down to nothing, only to be miraculously reconstituted. Back at the palace he tells a woman how to revive her son's dead ox. Now King Tranquillinus asks for another miracle, and George causes 17 souls, 460 years dead, to rise from their tomb, and baptizes them. After the strange 'poor widow episode', George is burnt to death and left on top of a mountain. Revived yet again he calls to the soldiers who brought him there and they are baptized into the faith.

When King Dacian tries persuasion, George pretends to give way, and converts Queen Alexandra. With the aid of the poor widow's son he destroys Apollo and smashes the other pagan idols. The queen is executed for her faith, after being hung by her breasts and burnt with torches. Finally, after a lengthy prayer for vengeance on his foes and for aid to all those who invoke his name, George is sentenced to death. When he is beheaded, water and milk flow from his body, and, in a close parallel with the death of Jesus, there is an earthquake, accompanied by thunder and lightning. This version is presented as the account of 'Passecras', George's servant, who was an eyewitness of all seven years of George's passion, and can confirm that no fewer than 30,900 people were converted (not counting the queen).

The ninth-century *Codex Sangallensis* gives a version that is very closely parallel to this – so much so, in fact, that they are thought to be independent translations of the same Greek original.

In point of fact there was no Empress or Queen Alexandra at this time. But who was Dacian? Various solutions have been put forward. Might he be the Emperor Decius (249–51)? The tenth-century *Chronicon Paschale* related that in the 255th year after the Assumption of Jesus Christ (i.e. during the reign of Diocletian) there was a great persecution, and among the many martyred were Sts George and Babylus. But the latter was certainly Bishop of Antioch from 237 to 250, and if, as tradition has it, Diocletian sent a force to destroy a church containing relics of St George, then the saint clearly died some time earlier.[8]

Another guess is that Dacian might be Galerius (emperor 293–311), who was from Dacia (modern Romania), and might therefore have been called 'Dacianus', 'the Dacian'. Galerius was appointed Caesar of the East in 293, and it was he more than any other who urged Diocletian to persecute the Christians. Others have thought that Dacian was the Emperor Maximinus, whom Diocletian made Caesar of the East in 305, and whose surname was Daza. Or Dacian could merely be a rationalization of a Persian name: it is not clear whether he was a local governor, or a king, or the emperor. At least we seem to be in the right period.

So much for the Greek and Latin traditions. They stem ultimately from the same Greek original, and follow the same broad outlines, but with much variation of detail. They will strike modern readers as incredible on many counts, but if they compare them with the endlessly expanded versions that found favour in the East, and those that were later current in medieval England, they will soon regard them as comparatively credible.

And while on the subject of incredibility, it may be useful at this point to say something of the tortures to which George was subjected. Some of them are clearly both historically accurate and feasible (e.g. scourging, or the rack): others are so elaborate and implausible as to seem ludicrous. Clearly torture-descriptions were good copy and, while serving to glorify a saint, might at the same time satisfy all sorts of other needs.

The Lives describe George as broken on a wheel. No two artists have pictured this wheel-torture in exactly the same way: some have shown the saint bound to two wheels and about to be wrenched apart; others have gone for a single wheel with knives attached either to it, or to a platform beneath. St Euphemia faced a similarly ingenious device – so ingenious, in fact, that it destroyed the executioners. St Catherine, about to be mangled by four nail-studded wheels, was saved when an angel smashed the device (which seems to have happened in some visual cycles of St George).

Nearly all the tortures George suffers can be paralleled in the lives of other saints: John the Evangelist was made to drink poison; Thomas was thrown into a furnace; Vincent and Ignatius were raked with iron combs; Justina was plunged into a cauldron of boiling pitch (a process described by Josephus during the torturing of the Maccabees); Blaise and Margaret had plates and hooks driven into their bodies. Occasionally interesting variations are introduced, perhaps reflecting local traditions or the demands of individual patrons.

The horrid truth is that not so many of the tortures described are as fictional as the reader might fancy or wish. Caligula had a man sawn in two; Trajan burned Polycarp alive; Decius and Valerian had Christians dragged at the horse's tail, scourged, scalded with boiling oil and lead and mutilated to death.

George's stoical silence during his suffering must in part at least be put down to the zeal of the hagiographer. But in the 1626 *Compendium Maleficiarum* it is recorded that a 50-year-old woman endured boiling fat poured over her and severe racking without a murmur, though her big toe was torn off in the process. (It was sincerely believed that God would lend the innocent strength to endure any amount of torture.) The 'red hot boot' was used in the sixteenth century; and the 'iron boot' (into which wedges were driven until the bones were crushed) was employed on a man accused of trying to assassinate the Duke of York in 1681, while His Grace and other worthies looked on.

Having sampled the Greek and Latin Acta the reader will have seen how, onto the primitive and authentic record, material was grafted that either belongs elsewhere or simply belongs to the realms of fancy. The purest, earliest form of the legend would simply have been a record of the life and death of a Christian martyr, written by Christians for the instruction and edification of other Christians. The early Acta, of course, deal only with the passion of St George: the dragon episode was not recorded until much later.[9]

The purpose of a Life is to establish the hero's sanctity: the grimmer and more extensive the tortures he endured, therefore, the more heroic his endurance, the better. If in the Middle Ages among the better educated there was a tendency to expurgate and trim the elements that smacked of heresy or were too patently absurd, as the cultus spread there was also a movement towards elaboration and hyperbole. Even a brief glance at the longer eastern Lives will show how, among the seemingly inexhaustible variety of tortures to which the saints were subjected, it became

21

almost impossible to invent anything new, and in an attempt to prove George's supreme status among martyrs his hagiographers dreamt up procedures that are either incomprehensible or ludicrous, or both at once. As Delehaye has put it, 'it is only when they are at the end of their own resources that the writers allow their heroes to die'.[10]

Of the eastern texts the Syrian and Coptic (Egyptian) manuscripts are the earliest, and they were translated from a Greek original no longer extant. The Arabic version follows the Coptic very closely, and the Ethiopic is derived from the Coptic and Arabic versions. The reader who is determined to study these oriental Lives can find them, in all their bewildering complexity, conveniently translated in a single, fat volume.[11]

The short Syriac version is supposedly the eyewitness account of our friend pseudo-Pasicrates: the martyrdom is dated precisely to the twenty-third day of Nisan (April) at the seventh hour on the eve of the Sabbath (Friday). The Coptic version is composed of three separate works: a life by 'Pasicrates', an account of nine miracles performed by George during the translation of his remains, and an encomium delivered on his feast day – an elaborate, much expanded version of the passion and death which amalgamates several other current legends of the saint. Most scholars believe that these last two documents, though ancient, are spurious.

But what is new? We are given various biographical details of George (e.g. he is from Melitene in Cappadocia, and his mother is daughter of the Count of Diospolis), the odd romantic flourish (he is betrothed to the governor's daughter) and much hagiographical amplification – conversions on an even grander scale, even more impossibly vile tortures, and more miraculous revivals. 'Pasicrates' also tells us of events after George's execution: the removal of his corpse to Lydda, the building of a shrine there, and his subsequent appearance to the Emperor Constantine, resulting in the construction of an even more magnificent shrine. And so on.

The Arabic Life is very similar, as is the Ethiopic, the latter providing copious details of George's martyrdom; endless lists, lovingly detailed, of all the tyrant's implements of torture; and apparently verbatim transcripts of the dialogue between the tyrant and the saint, in which we see the author trying his best to make the 'facts' of the legend more appealing to his audience. At the beginning of this account Christ tells George he must suffer for seven years and die four times. When finally they turn the last blood-soaked page, even the most devoted readers will feel that they too know something of suffering.

We have come a long way from the simple story of a man of eastern provenance who was probably martyred around the end of the third century AD. The basic 'facts' have been mythified, and in the full-blown Life we can see a mêlée of different material employed indiscriminately to emphasize the physical suffering of the martyr, his superhuman endurance, his examination and triumph, the resulting conversions, the punishment of his oppressors, and his ultimate vindication.

We have come a long way but we have further to go. Soon our fearless hero becomes a knight and finds himself in Libya rescuing a damsel from a fire-breathing dragon. But now it is time to look at events closer to home.

First, George comes to England.

NOTES

1 Other cities cited as places of his execution are Melitene in Cappadocia, Tyre in Phoenicia (Lebanon) and Nicomedia in Bithynia.
2 *Historia Ecclesiastica* VIII 5.
3 Though some recent scholars have declared it spurious, Pope Gelasius' Index of Forbidden Books is almost universally accepted as genuine.
4 Cod. Athen. 422 (dated 1546).
5 Cod. Vat. 1660 (dated 916).
6 H. Delehaye, SJ, *The Legends of the Saints*, pp. 70f.
7 Fr Herbert Thurston, 'St George', p. 477.
8 This was the view of Wallis Budge, who put George's death around 250/1 AD.
9 One must distinguish between visual and literary records. The first written account of the dragon-conflict seems to be in the thirteenth-century *Golden Legend* of Jacobus de Voragine. See Chapter 4.
10 Delehaye, *Legends of the Saints*, p. 97.
11 Sir E. A. Wallis Budge, *George of Lydda, The Patron Saint of England*.

3

ST GEORGE IN ENGLAND:
THE MEDIEVAL TRADITION

After his martyrdom the cult of St George spread rapidly through the Christian East. (It reached northern Syria by the fifth century, and Egypt probably by the sixth, and was carried to Rome and Gaul by merchants and pilgrims returning from Jerusalem and Constantinople.) He is referred to by St Ambrose of Milan (fourth century), by the historian Procopius (sixth century), and by St Gregory, Bishop of Tours and historian of the Franks (sixth century). Ambrose talks of George as the 'most faithful servant of Jesus Christ'; and the celebrated Latin poet Venantius Fortunatus (*c*.530–*c*.610) in his *De Basilica Sancti Georgii* makes a significant reference to his importance as an intercessor in the West.

Soon after his death, too, his body was divided for relics, and by the seventh century most, if not all, of it had been distributed to satisfy the demand of the faithful. Gregory of Tours tells us that George's body was preserved in a church near Ramleh (close to Lydda): the body (minus its head) was buried in the middle of the choir. Caxton records that the Emperor Sigismund sent the heart of St George to Henry V, who placed it in St George's Chapel, Windsor, where at other times a skull of St George was kept, and three of his (unspecified) bones were preserved in a silver reliquary. A part of one leg was bequeathed by Henry VIII in his will. An arm was owned by the Guild of St George at Norwich and kept in the cathedral there.

In the eighth century Pope Zacharias discovered St George's head in St John Lateran, where surely it must have lain from earliest times for it to have been so completely forgotten. He solemnly presented it to the ancient church of San Giorgio in Velabro from where it passed in time to the church of San Giorgio, Ferrara. (At Ferrara George seems to have enjoyed a special cult, and in the new cathedral built there in the twelfth century, there was an arm of St George, thought to have been a gift from Robert Count of Flanders to Countess Mathilda.)

One recent writer attests the existence of no fewer than five different heads, or pieces of head. Other heads are recorded at Reichenau, in Syria and at Marmoutier, and an entire skull is preserved in the abbey of San Giorgio Maggiore on the island of San Giorgio, Venice. King Edward IV gave a head of the saint 'with a helmet of gold' to the chapel at Windsor. The author of the *Acta Sanctorum* lists many other relics of St George in far-flung places, in Fulda, Cambrai, Prague, Toulouse, Bologna, Naples and Palermo, for example, including yet another head in Syracuse. But before dismissing all apparently duplicated relics as obvious fakes, one should bear in mind that reliquaries very often take the shape of the whole limb or organ of which the enclosed relic is part (a piece of finger may appear in a hand-shaped reliquary), and that there was no doubt a tendency to take all relics labelled 'George' as relics of the most celebrated George.

Gregory of Tours writes of the special veneration of relics of the saint in France. The existence of a bone from the saint's arm is recorded very early at St Germain des Prés. In the late medieval period the area of the greatest devotion to the saint was undoubtedly Normandy, where his cult was developed well before it became established in England. In the late medieval period in Normandy alone nearly 70 churches were dedicated to him, as well as guilds and confraternities, and there were fairs and healing springs and wells associated with St George. And in the mid eighth century we have a contemporary chronicle relating the miraculous arrival on the shore of Portbail, on the north-west coast of the Cotentin peninsula, of a container shaped like a miniature lighthouse (*turricula*) which, when it was opened, revealed a most beautiful copy of the Gospels in Latin, and a reliquary containing part of the jawbone of St George, as well as other precious relics, including wood from the Holy Cross. (In the reliquary were letters of authentication for each of these.) The locals were astounded and a day of fasting was proclaimed. The container was then placed on a wagon pulled by two cows and everyone awaited the pleasure of the Almighty. At once the cows took off at a trot and came to the place called Brix, where the local grandee (Count Richwin) organized not only the building of a basilica to St George, but also two others, one dedicated to the Virgin and the other to the Holy Cross. In the basilica the precious relic was duly placed (together, according to the chronicler, with yet another head of the martyr), and countless miracles were performed there.

The provenance of this gift of God was never ascertained. The writer, knowing that Pope Zacharias had discovered the skull of St George in Rome, wondered if some pilgrims, possibly British, had been presented with these relics by the Pope in Rome, and been subsequently shipwrecked on the return journey. (But the precise dating of St George's arrival in England is unknown. He was certainly known to St Gregory (Pope from 590) who was, through St Augustine and his team of missionaries, responsible for the re-establishment of the Church in England. The earliest reference to St George in Anglo-Saxon literature comes at the very beginning of the eighth century.) Or perhaps some Italian or French church, situated near the sea, had been flooded and lost this tower-shaped object, which was on the large side for the convenient carriage of relics (8 feet tall, and 3 feet wide at the base) and might have been a piece of church furniture.

It is commonly said that George came over to England with the Crusaders, but though unquestionably his cult in the East and the stories of his miraculous appearances enhanced his popularity, he was known in this country as early as the seventh century. Bede (c.673–735) states in his martyrology that George suffered under Datian (or Dacian), the Persian king, and lists his feast day on 23 April. But probably the first mention of the saint comes in the *De Locis Sanctis* of Adamnan, Abbot of Iona (c.625–704), which describes the pilgrimage to Palestine of a certain bishop named

Arculf(us) around the year 700. Arculf had seen the statue of St George in the church at Lydda.

Of the many churches dedicated to St George in this country, the oldest is probably that at Fordington, Dorset, which is mentioned in the will of Alfred the Great. The church has a carved tympanum dated to around 1100 depicting St George as a Crusader; he is mounted on horseback with a lance. There is a similar Norman carving at Damerham near Fordingbridge, Hants, where George (if it is he) is pictured on horseback, wielding a sword and trampling on the enemy. How St George became a knight in the first place is not clear, but his miraculous appearances to troops at the sieges of Antioch and Jerusalem will perhaps have aided the connection.

The cult of St George predates the First Crusade (1095) by two to three centuries at least. A monastery dedicated to George had been founded at Thetford in Norfolk before the time of Canute (1017–35), and there was certainly a St George's Church in Southwark in the Anglo-Saxon period, and another at Windsor before the First Crusade.

Aelfric, the 'Grammarian', a great scholar and the most celebrated literary figure of his day, composed a metrical Life of St George among his 'Lives of the Saints' (993–8) while a monk at Cerne Abbas in Dorset, and since it is with him that the English tradition of George begins, it may be worth looking at his poem in some detail.

Aelfric begins by acknowledging the existence of false, heretical versions of the story, and declaring that his own version will be the truth. George was 'a rich noble under the cruel emperor . . . called Dacian, in the shire of Cappadocia'. Appalled by the heathen's devil-worship, George gives away his property to the poor and boldly tells the emperor: '*Omnes dii gentium demonia: dominus autem caelos fecit*' (Psalm 96.5: 'All the gods of the nations are devils, but the LORD made the heavens'). Dacian, 'fiendishly' angered, asks George who he is and what 'borough' he is from. George tells him his name and the country of his birth, where he is in a position of some authority. Dacian requires him to sacrifice

27

to Apollo, but George 'interrogates' the 'fiendish' emperor, who with 'devilish' anger has him hung upon a gibbet, his limbs torn with iron claws and his sides burnt with torches. He is then taken out of the city and scourged, and his wounds are rubbed with salt. When George emerges from this unhurt, he is thrown into prison.

Dacian now seeks the aid of a sorcerer, and Athanasius comes forward, promising to overcome the holy man. Dacian tells George he must either overcome his magic or be overcome by it. Athanasius mixes a noxious draught for George, but when this fails to poison him, declares that if he fails a second time he will submit to Christ. George drinks the 'fiendish liquor' without turning a hair and when Athanasius begs him for baptism, George obliges him.

Dacian is now 'fiendishly' angry, and has Athanasius taken out of the city and beheaded. (All this appears to have taken place on the first day – a day crowded with incident.)

On the second day Dacian commands George to be bound on a broad wheel 'and two sharp swords to be set against him, / and so to be drawn up, and shoved backwards'. George asks for God's help, and the wheel bursts apart before it can be used to harm him.

Dacian is now determined to destroy George. A cauldron full of boiling lead is fetched, and George, making the sign of the cross over it, lies in it, 'and the lead was cooled through God's might'.

Dacian now changes tack and offers to shower George with honours if he sacrifices to Apollo. George, filled with the Holy Ghost, 'smiles with his mouth', and remarks ambiguously: 'It befitteth us that we sacrifice to the immortal god.' Dacian is fooled by his apparent compliance and has his temples richly adorned for the sacrifice George will make. But George on bended knee asks God to shatter the miserable images, 'even as wax melteth before a hot fire'. Suddenly fire falls from heaven, the temple is consumed and the idols and their priests fall into the earth never to reappear.

George is quick to point out the uselessness of idol-worship to Dacian, who finally loses all patience and sentences him to death. He is to be dragged 'prone with his face to the earth' through all the streets of the city and the rough paths out of the city, and put to the sword.

George is taken to the place of execution, and in prayer gives thanks to God for all his mercies, and for giving him the victory. He also prays for rain 'because the heat was then wasting the land'. After his execution some countrymen of his, fellow Christians, take up his body and bury him honourably in the city.

In answer to George's prayer the Lord sends rain, and Dacian and his companions, as they return home, are destroyed by fire from heaven. While George wings his way to Christ to dwell with him in glory, Aelfric remarks, with grim humour, that Dacian was in hell before he even got home again.

Aelfric has put into Anglo-Saxon verse an account of the Acta which is at once familiar, and also comparatively sober. (It represents, surely, a certain amount of rationalization and expurgation of his original.) There is no dragon, of course, nor any empress or governor's wife for George to convert. George is a holy man, a rich noble, not a knight, nor even a soldier. The story of a dauntless martyr overcoming the menace of a heathen tyrant is a stirring one, and must surely have struck a chord in the hearts of the Anglo-Saxons, who had continually to face the raids of the pagan Vikings.

But if George was known in England before the Norman Conquest, it was during the Crusades that he became pre-eminent. He could indeed be called the patron of the Crusades. He had appeared to Normans fighting Sicilian Muslims at Cerami in 1063 in shining armour, mounted on a white charger, and with a white banner with a cross flying from his lance. William of Malmesbury, in his *Gesta Regum Anglorum* (finished c.1136) records that George was first adopted as patron saint by the soldiers of Robert II, Duke of Normandy, son of the Conqueror, during the First Crusade. At the Battle of Antioch in June 1098 when the Crusaders faced ignominious defeat, knights appeared on white horses clad in white with white shields and banners and led them to victory. The Turks had surrounded the Crusaders and were picking them off with arrows and spears, when the white army suddenly appeared from the hills around them. The standard bearers were identified as Sts George, Demetrius and Maurice (or Theodore, or Mercurius). The event is also attested by other contemporary historians. When the Crusaders pushed on to Lydda, there was no sign of the Saracens, who had left the place in a great hurry, and as a result, in gratitude to George, Lydda was elevated to the level of a see. George was also to aid the Crusaders at the siege of Jerusalem. (He wore white armour with a red cross on it, and commanded an army of angels.) The walls were scaled and the city taken on 15 July 1099. One account says that on this occasion he was accompanied by St Maurice and 30,000 knights; another puts the figure at 100,000 men. Such events were no doubt regarded as miraculous by the English, but the Syrians and Palestinians had for some 2,000 years expected their God to be present and to help them in battle (see e.g. 2 Maccabees 3.24, 25; 5.2, 3; 10.29; 11.8). Nor were these St George's last appearances: he was to be seen aiding British troops in France (as the Maid of Orleans was thought to have inspired French troops) in the First World War, and a host of angels were seen fighting at the side of the British forces at Mons.

Many such tales were brought back to the West by those returning from the Crusades, and in post-Conquest England the example shown by St George, as well as reports of his miraculous powers as intercessor, may well have exercised a strong appeal to a people whose culture and traditions were being systematically and ruthlessly suppressed by the Normans.

In the Third Crusade, when Richard the Lionheart was in Palestine (1191–2) he is said to have discovered the martyr's tomb at Lydda, and as the result of a vision of St George to have placed himself and his troops under the saint's protection. Some traditions state that he rebuilt the cathedral (erected between 1150 and 1170 on the site of the original church of Constantine) which had been destroyed by Saladin in 1191. But it is unlikely that it was in fact Richard I who established the English monarchy's special cult of St George. It was certainly Edward I (1272–1307), Richard's great-nephew, who began the practice of flying the banner of St George alongside those of St Edmund and St Edward the Confessor. It is also known that a red cross flag was carried by troops under Henry III at the Battle of Evesham (1265), but it is not certain if this was actually the banner of St George, or just the opposite of the Angevin white cross flag used by de Montfort and the rebel army. In 1277, during Edward I's campaign against the Welsh, we have our first definite reference to the banner of St George. Accounts for that year detail payments to the king's tailor for the purchase of material for the making of pennoncels (streamers for lances) and bracers (armour for the forearm) of the arms of St George.

The banner of St George is the red Greek cross of a martyr on a ground of white (argent, a cross, gules). In Byzantium the use of the military banner of St George and St Michael and other warrior saints dates back to the tenth century and predates its adoption in the West by two centuries. Though some writers believe it was actually William the Conqueror who first flew the red cross of St George from his masthead as he sailed to Britain, and that he fought under it on Senlac Hill at the Battle of Hastings, it is generally believed that it was Richard I who first used the banner for his army, and Richard II who established it as the army's flag. But it was Edward III who, by dedicating the chapel at Windsor to St George in 1348, began the move away from St Edward the Confessor and towards St George as our patron saint. During his campaign in France Edward's men at arms wore the red cross; and when Richard II invaded Scotland in 1385, his men were ordered to display the arms of St George 'before and behind'. The red cross flag was flown by English ships from the thirteenth century onwards. From the mid fourteenth century the red cross banner became the official arms of the City of London (later two dragons were added as supporters), with an upward-pointing red sword (the sword of St Paul, patron saint of London) in its first quarter. The red cross banner also appears in the arms of the cities of Durham, Lincoln, Rochester and York.

It was, of course, Edward III who founded the Most Noble Order of the Garter, naming George (with the Holy Trinity, the Blessed Virgin Mary and St Edward the Confessor) as its patron.

The origins of the Order are obscure. Some say it was Richard I who told his own troops to tie blue thongs to their legs as a novel mark of distinction, and promised to make any who succeeded in scaling the walls of Jerusalem 'Companions of St George'. The battle cries 'For George!', 'St George forward!' or 'Upon them St George!' became ways of stirring the Crusaders to renewed efforts when the going was hard. Others think the garter may be derived from the girdle worn by the princess whom George rescued from the dragon. The popular legend is that the beautiful Countess of Salisbury lost her garter accidentally at a court ball, and King Edward, retrieving it, gallantly tied it to his own knee with the remark: '*Honi soit qui mal y pense*' ('Evil to him who thinks evil of it'). It was this incident, the story goes, that caused him to abandon his plan of establishing an Order of the Round Table, and to institute in its stead the Order of the Garter.

By the end of the fourteenth century St George was firmly accepted as patron saint of England. The association of St George with the Order of the Garter[1] gave a further stimulus to his popularity in England, and in the next century and a half a great number of churches were dedicated to him; guilds and other institutions affiliated to his cult were founded up and down the country. George had become the patron of knights and of chivalry, protector of holy places and the Crusaders. He symbolized England's championing of the cause of Christendom.

Mention has been made of the two early churches of St George at Fordington and Damerham. Frescoes of St George are still visible in some 50 village churches in England. The earliest are in Sussex, and dated *c.*1080–1120. The most spectacular are at St Botolph's Church at Hardham near Pulborough in West Sussex. Among the tiered paintings which cover the walls, on the lower tier of the north wall, west of the door, is one which is believed to show the apparition of St George to the Crusaders at Antioch in 1098. He is on a white charger, wearing a skull cap and spearing an enemy knight with a long lance. Other scenes show him on trial and on the wheel. These precious frescoes are thought to be the work of artists from the Cluniac Priory of St Pancras at Lewes.

The oldest carved image of St George in England is that at Fordington, and its dating makes it more or less contemporaneous with the apparition at Antioch depicted at Hardham. The Fordington George is in fact unarmed, but haloed, and thrusts a lance with red cross pennant into the mouth of a fallen foe; the dead bodies lie before him in a trampled heap, while behind two Crusaders kneel in prayer. At Damerham, George charges, sword in hand, and tramples on the enemy. (In both these carvings, interestingly, we can see the enemy depicted in attitudes which are reminiscent of those of the dragon in later iconography.) George had become a great Christian knight. Like other warrior saints (e.g. Sts Mercury, Menas, Demetrius, Theodore) he is pictured on horseback, in the established iconographic idiom. Much that would have been of vital importance in this study was destroyed during the Reformation and Commonwealth, but much still remains, and some of the later images of our saint will be reviewed when we come to consider the dragon motif in Chapter 4.

So England claimed George as her own[2] and the story of England's veneration of the saint has its own special history. The telling and retelling of George's heroic deeds, especially during the late medieval period, produced many interesting variations on the original theme. Legend has it that George, a tribune in the Roman army, actually visited Britain on the orders of Diocletian, and became friendly with Helena, Empress of Britain, the daughter of King Cole of East Britain ('Old King Cole'). This, some even claimed, was none other than St Helena, the mother of Constantine the Great, who discovered the true cross, built a church to St George on the site of his execution, and also erected the first church to St George at Jerusalem near the Church of the Holy Sepulchre. This identification, ridiculed by Gibbon,[3] was perpetrated in the first instance by Geoffrey of Monmouth in his *History of the Kings of Britain*. In fact George (goes the story) had served with the future Emperor Constantine on both the Persian and Egyptian expeditions under Galerius, and formed a lasting friendship with him. George, while in this country, visited Glastonbury, to pay his respects to the tomb of his relative Joseph of Arimathea, and Caerleon-on-

Usk, an early centre of Christianity. Indeed, as we shall see, the dragon was said to be of pure English origin, and a number of widely dispersed places claim to be the site of the famous conflict.

Constantine's name is indelibly associated with that of George. It was Constantine, the first Christian emperor, who used the symbol of the cross on the *labarum* (legionary standard); it was to become the symbol of Christianity against paganism. Constantine is also said to have rewarded his soldiers for acts of bravery with a gold collar with a pendant cross – a replica of the one that had appeared to him at the Battle of the Milvian Bridge in 312 bearing the legend *IN HOC SIGNO VINCES* ('Under this sign you shall prevail'). In 312 Constantine may have founded the first known order of knighthood under the patronage of St George; and in 314 at the Council of Arles, according to the tradition of the Greek Church, Constantine proposed that George of Lydda should become the model of young Christian manhood and be known as 'the Champion Knight of Christendom'. Constantine dedicated some 20 churches to St George, among them a great Byzantine edifice on the site of the shrine which housed his remains. The name and figure of Constantine the Great features largely in the legend of St George: in many respects Constantine might be described as his human analogue. Intriguingly, the fourth-century historian Eusebius relates that Constantine had an image made of himself overcoming a dragon, a symbol of the devil, and such an image is thought to have been displayed in the church he built over George's shrine at Lydda.

Sooner or later a tradition was bound to arise that George was in fact a native of his country of adoption.[4] In one late sixteenth-century romance George becomes a native of Coventry (a far cry from Lydda). But more of that later. In England, as we see, there was a very healthy tradition of tinkering with the canonical 'facts' of the tale, both for the sake of a good story and in the interests of patriotism.

But the dragon keeps rearing its ugly head, and can only be ignored in the story of St George for so long.

1   See Chapter 5.
2   Though not England alone. St George is patron saint of many other countries. At various stages of history Venice, Genoa, Portugal, Aragon, Catalonia, Georgia, Moscow and Istanbul have adopted him as their special protector.
3   'This tradition, unknown to the contemporaries of Constantine, was invented in the darkness of monasteries, was embellished by Jeffrey [sic] of Monmouth and the writers of the twelfth century...' *Decline and Fall*, Folio Society edn, 1983, vol. II, p. 57.
4   St George's Channel, the stretch of water between Wales and Ireland, gets its name from the late legend that the saint travelled to England.

4

ENTER THE DRAGON

So in due course George became a knight and killed a dragon.

Everyone knows what a dragon is: dragons are common to almost every culture. A dragon is a huge monster with large and sharp teeth, gaping jaws, fiery and pestilential breath and cruel talons: a dragon is scaly, has wings and sometimes a forked tail. It is a sort of dinosaur-cum-crocodile, a winged serpent – everything that is terrifying and repellent to humankind, its loathsome curly tail reminiscent of the serpent which was the cause of Man's Fall in the Garden of Eden. The Christian regards the serpent as the embodiment of evil.

Sources are at variance over the precise timing of the dragon's entry into the story of George. But it is certainly a late addition, and its relation to the martyrdom story is uncertain.[1]

Are dragons purely fictitious, just fabulous heraldic beasts, or did they exist once and then die out? Or are they simply exaggerated descriptions of real wild beasts (imaginative reconstructions of exhumed dinosaur remains, perhaps) or possibly even collective psychical manifestations? Whatever the answer, they are one of the most ancient of beasts, referred to originally in Mesopotamian cultures, in the Old and New Testaments, in the stories of the desert fathers and in European romances. Medieval belief in them seems to have been commonplace: they appeared in bestiaries, in church windows, in Dooms on the chancel crossing. Dragons also appear on many ancient seals: those of Basingstoke, Linlithgow, Dumfries and Hastings show St Michael killing a dragon; and on the old corporation seal of Lynn Regis (now King's Lynn) St Margaret stands upon a dragon wounding it with a cross.

Countless sightings of dragons have been recorded in the course of history. One was seen in 1170 at St Osyth, Essex, for example. In 1233 a pair were seen fighting in the sky off the south coast. In 1395 a dragon ran amok over many areas of England; and in the early fifteenth century there was a sighting near Bures in West Suffolk. In the fifteenth century the heir of the Lambton family caught a snakelike creature in the River Wear and flung it into a well in disgust. In no time at all the dragon grew and grew until it settled on the north bank of the Wear a mile from Lambton Castle. It was so huge now that it wrapped itself three times around a small hill, which received the imprints of its coils. In true dragon fashion the Lambton Worm ravaged the countryside, blighted crops and devoured livestock, and whenever it was attacked and wounded, its flesh was magically healed. Young Lambton sought the advice of a witch, who told him to wear armour with razors attached to it, and promised that he would win a victory if he swore to kill the first living thing he met after his battle with the Worm. This he vowed to do; he killed the dragon and sounded his horn in triumph – a prearranged signal for his greyhound to be released, so that he could fulfil his oath by killing it. But his father forgot the plan and ran to greet his son. Killing the greyhound subsequently was not enough: the Lambton family were cursed for nine generations.

And during the seventeenth century there was a celebrated dragon loose in St Leonard's Forest near Horsham in Sussex (an area still eerie with associations). There was a most famous dragon of Wantley (Wharncliffe, in the West Riding of Yorkshire); the Laidley Worm of Bamburgh Castle; the medieval serpent of Handale in Yorkshire; and dragons have been recorded at various periods at Bignor Hill in Sussex, flying between Cadbury Camp and Dolebury Hill in Clevedon, at Linton Hill a few miles from Kelso, at Ludham in Norfolk, and at Mordiford in Herefordshire. Today we have the Yeti of Tibet, the Loch Ness monster, the Sasquatch of Canada, and the Ogopogo which lives in the Okanagan Lake in British Columbia. Belief in fabulous creatures is far from dead.

Dragons are closely linked with water, and they were often seen infesting lakes and rivers. Fifty yards north of the church at Lyminster, near Arundel in Sussex, is the notorious 'Knucker Hole' (*Nicor* is Saxon for 'sea monster'), a 'bottomless' pool which 1,200–1,500 years ago was haunted by a terrible dragon. When the king offered his daughter in marriage to any man brave enough to kill the monster many tried and lost their lives. Then a young hero arrives, sails into the Arun, slays the dragon and marries the princess: his gravestone can still be seen to the left of the pool.

There is a 'dragon's well' south of the church at Brinsop in Herefordshire, and over the door of the church there is a carving of St George and the dragon. In Wales there are several wells (Grinston Well in Dyfed, for example, and Serpent Well in Gwynedd) associated with dragons.

Our dragon, the one St George fights, is no doubt based in some measure on biblical prototypes: on Leviathan, described in Job as a huge, scaly, fire-breathing sea monster; on the unnamed monster Daniel dispatches in the apocryphal Bel and the Dragon; and the dragon in Revelation, with which St Michael does battle, which he casts down on the earth and which is named Satan. The dragon is the Ancient Enemy.

Some have identified the dragon of St George's story with the evil Dacian, who is more than once called a 'serpent' and 'dragon' in the oriental texts. Others see the conflict between George and the dragon as symbolic of the primeval struggle between light and darkness, good and evil, orthodoxy and heresy, the higher and the lower nature. There are many pre-Christian tales of conflicts between heroes and monsters, and it may be that St George's struggle is an echo of these ancient pagan confrontations. Killing dragons was the hero's job: heroes slew monsters. Perseus slew Medusa; Jason killed the dragon that guarded the golden fleece. Sumerian and Babylonian tradition tells of Marduk, champion of the gods, killing the dragon Tiamat ('wrong', 'chaos'). Hebrew tradition had Daniel overcoming a dragon; Christian, in *Pilgrim's Progress*, Beowulf and Siegfried did the same. The Easterners would naturally attribute to St George some of the feats of their other great national leaders, and indeed it is possible that in early times in the East those venerating his cult may have thought that George was part God and part human. (Wallis Budge compares Gilgamesh, King of Erech, who was two-thirds god and one-third human, and suggests that, if George were somewhat similarly endowed, this might possibly explain his four deaths and three revivals.) The Arabs saw George as an incarnation of Moses or Elijah, and there is a legend, possibly common to Arabs and Christians, of one Girgis (or Jirjis) Bakiya ('the resurrected one'), a prophet who was killed several times but raised to life again by God; and another tradition of Al Khidr ('the Green One') whose soul passed through Elijah and St George, a prophet and warrior who drank of the water of the well of life and became (green and) immortal. Al Khidr, always a champion of Jews and Christians against the heathen, led them in battle, and aided the Crusaders in the person of St George.

Perhaps St George was confused with other dragon-slayers: with the Egyptian Horus, who kills a crocodile, a scaly and very dragon-like animal, or St Michael, who with his angels fought with the dragon, 'that old serpent, called the Devil';[2] or with St Margaret, St Silvester and St Martha, all of whom are depicted as overcoming dragons. St George is very often paired with St Michael. The Virgin, too, is often shown trampling on a serpent, and George's association with the Virgin becomes increasingly strong in medieval times (the church built by the grateful king whose city has been saved from the dragon is dedicated, significantly, to the Virgin and St George). Just possibly St George was confused with the bas relief described in the church of St George at Lydda, representing Constantine standing triumphantly upon a serpent. Over 100 medieval saints were credited with the slaying of dragons, but none was English. Perhaps this fact, as well as the fact that his martyrdom fell in the period given over to the Rogations (when the dragon as the emblem of winter was carried in processions through Christendom to mark the beginning of spring) helped St George to become one of their number.

It may be useful at this point briefly to remind the reader of the story as it is told in *The Golden Legend*. A city called Silene in

Libya is terrorized by a dragon which infests a vast lake and must be fed if it is to be kept at bay. (Note the connection of the dragon with water; this is not only the water essential to life and civilization, but it is the water of baptism. The dragon is the enemy of the true faith.) At first it is given sheep, but when these run out, the citizens resort to feeding it a man and a sheep; then, apparently at the king's command, lots are cast to decide which of the young people (why the young?) are to be the dragon's victims. Finally the lot falls on the king's own daughter. The king tries to buy his way out of trouble, but the citizens are adamant and he is obliged to comply with their demands. His daughter is led to the appointed place and in due course St George rides by. The princess tries to dissuade him from his reckless bravery, but George does battle with the dragon and wounds it. To the horror of the citizens, the maiden leads the beast into the city by her girdle and, when the citizens agree to be baptized, George slays the dragon with his sword. A church is dedicated by the grateful king, and George, after refusing rewards and giving the king some parting advice, goes on his way.

Now what St George is doing in Libya is not clear (one version explains his presence by stating that he has been sent there on the orders of Diocletian) and other places as far apart as Beirut and Dunsmore Heath have claimed to be the true site of the encounter. Silene could perhaps be the corrupted form of some real city in North Africa, such as Cyrene.[3]

As already stated, the legend of George and the dragon (with a king and queen and princess) was popularized by Voragine's *The Golden Legend* (*c.*1260), but the dragon-story did not begin with Voragine, who was a compiler, not an inventor, of tales. The dragon-motif occurs much earlier, for example in the sixth/seventh-century terracotta icons found in Macedonia and Tunisia in the 1980s, one showing St Theodore lancing a serpent, and another Sts George and Christopher each spearing a serpent with human head. Moscow used a seal depicting St George and the dragon as its coat of arms as early as the ninth century, and there is an early tenth-century carving of the same subject in the church of St George, Prague. The conflict with the dragon has an extremely ancient tradition in North Africa, too, where St George is especially venerated by Christians and also by Muslims. There is also evidence linking the story to Old Egyptian and Phoenician sources.

The earliest visual reference in this country to the dragon episode is on an early twelfth-century tomb at St Peter's in Conisbrough, Yorkshire. The carving shows the princess already in the dragon's clutches, while an abbot nearby gives his blessing to her saviour.

The Golden Legend was subsequently translated into French in the fourteenth century by Jean de Vignay, then into English by an anonymous translator in a version called the *Gilte Legende* (1438). This is a close translation of the French version, though the author evidently had a Latin text in front of him as a control, and he also adds a few chapters not in the French. In the *Gilte Legende*, George is a 'iuge' (judge, Latin *iudex*, meaning 'governor') from Cappadocia. His presence in Libya is unexplained. The dragon infests a 'stange, a ponde' and is at first fed two sheep to keep it from killing off citizens with its foul breath. Then when the sheep begin to run out, it is given a sheep and a man, until finally the lot falls on the king's daughter. In royal attire (as in *The Golden Legend*, but not Caxton) the princess goes to her death. St George wounds the monster and the princess leads it into the city with her girdle about its neck, and it follows her meekly, 'as a debonayre hounde'. No fewer than 20,000 people are converted and baptized (an improvement of 5,000 on Caxton), not counting women and children.

The passion, which now follows, is set in the reign of 'Dioclician' and 'Maximyan'. 'Dacyen' is a 'provost' and does to death 20,000 Christians, neatly balancing the numbers of converts in Silene. George arrives, is interrogated, and states that he has come to Palestine by the will of God. He is tortured on what the translator calls the 'eculee', and explains as 'a crosse and the two ends fastened in the erthe'. (But surely this is Latin *equleus*, and means 'rack'.) St Peter heals him. The unsuccessful enchanter is not named. More tortures follow and fail, and Dioclician tries bribery.

George, replying 'with a smylinge chere', pretends to yield. The temple, its idols and priests are all consumed by fire. The Empress 'Alexandrine' and George are executed and Dacian and his cronies plummet to hell. There follow stories of immovable relics and George's epiphany to the priest before the siege of Jerusalem (as in *The Golden Legend*); and (as in Caxton) a brief account of the chapel at Ramys (Ramleh), between Jaffa and Jerusalem, where the saint's headless corpse is preserved, with those of his father, mother and uncle; the pardons won by pilgrims there, and the miraculous cures obtained by mad Saracens who are brave enough to plunge their hands into a hole in the tomb. (Caxton has a further few lines on St George and the Order of the Garter in England.)

When Caxton printed his translation of *The Golden Legend* in 1483 its popularity was immediate and the story of George and the dragon became more or less fixed and canonical. Caxton based his version on three manuscripts, one French (a copy of an expanded version of the de Vignay translation referred to above), one English (an expanded version of the *Gilte Legende*) and one Latin (unknown), and it generally follows Voragine's text closely. But among the many minor differences, one of the more interesting is that the princess, as she goes to meet the dragon, is dressed as a bride, a detail which occurs elsewhere only in a Legendary written in fourteenth-century Scottish dialect,[4] and in the early sixteenth-century version of Alexander Barclay. This is clearly a fifteenth-century development. Perhaps the king wishes to say farewell to his daughter looking her best and reminding him of the wedding to which he had so looked forward ('Now shall I never see thine espousals'); but more probably it belongs to a version where the virgin is offered to George as his bride. In the pre-Christian versions of this story, the hero always marries the princess he rescues. But George does not. He prefers saving souls to love and marriage. He redistributes the money he is given, and remains loyal to his ideal of chastity (a motif that will be considered later on).

The story of the damsel rescued from a dragon was thought by Emile Mâle to have arisen from a misunderstanding of some picture.[5] It was the eastern custom to represent idolatry as a monster: this convention the West adopted, and the dragon became a symbol associated with those saints who took Christianity into heathen countries. According to Mâle, the dragon was a metaphor invented by the clergy, and it always guards some area of water (a symbol of baptism). The princess stands for Cappadocia, which George won for Christ, but the dragon was in due course taken as literal, and 'a metaphor became a story'. To defeat a dragon was to crush heresy and plant the true faith.

Dean Stanley[6] believed that the legend of St George, the martyr of Cappadocia, has been incorporated with a legend of the Arian George of Cappadocia, who in 357 usurped the see of Alexandria and was in 361 deposed and murdered by the mob. This George's contest was for the Empress Alexandra (the Alexandrian Church) and his enemy was Athanasius (Bishop of Alexandria). As the legend developed George became a knight rescuing an Egyptian princess and Athanasius was transfigured into the dragon. This attractive theory is perhaps over-ingenious, but it seems very probable that features of the Arian George's martyrdom did resurface in the legend of our St George.

So the fight with the dragon became part of the story of George, and from being an adventitious on-grafting of no relevance to the passion of the saint, it became the most instantly recognizable feature of his legend. The dragon was always popular, partly perhaps because of already existing stories of encounters between heroes and dragons, like that of Beowulf. In any case, the true legend with its serious moral message had become a mere romance.

After *The Golden Legend*, the dragon-episode is prominent in all the English literary versions of the legend, though its position within the story varies. The earliest of these lives, the *South English Legendary* (thirteenth century) deals with the martyrdom only, but an early fifteenth-century fragment written in the northern dialect exists (originally, it seems, a complete version of the legend) which is a variant on the version of the *South English Legendary*, and recounts the dragon-story.[7]

George is a 'gude knyght', a 'hayly man' from 'Capodse'. A city in 'Lyby' called Gylona is infested by 'a wonder foule dragone . . . both uggely and grete'. It gets a ration of two sheep a day (evidently the going rate), then a child and a sheep while stocks last. When the lot falls on his daughter, the king is dismayed, but his people threaten to burn down his palace if he does not surrender his daughter. He is granted a week in which to mourn the child he had hoped to see royally wed, then he sends her off, in 'rych qwenes clethynge' to meet her end. Now George comes riding by, attacks the dragon and wounds it many times. The princess puts her girdle about its neck and it follows her meekly into the city, much to the terror of the people. First George baptizes the king and all his folk, then draws his sword and dispatches the dragon, whose corpse is drawn out of town by a team of eight oxen. Twenty-two thousand are baptized that day (not counting women and children) and a church is erected in honour of 'our swete lorde and sayn george'. This version closely follows *The Golden Legend*.

Where both the martyrdom and the dragon-combat are related (as e.g. in Caxton and Voragine) the dragon-episode is normally placed first, as would be expected, and the martyrdom is introduced abruptly. (In the Scottish Legendary, however, George rides off in haste to Persia in order to preach the Christian truths there.) In the *Speculum Sacerdotale*[8] however, the dragon-fight comes second – a disconcerting chronology, as George has by now been beheaded. The sudden transition to Libya, introduced by the words 'in a certeyne time', leaves the relationship of this section to the preceding one vague. All this took place *before*, we are to imagine, at some unspecified time in George's life.

In John Mirk's *Festial*,[9] a collection of sermons for the festivals of the Christian year, dated *c*. 1400, the conflict with the 'horrybull dragon' comes first, but without any information as to which country or city it is terrorizing. After George has slain it and converted the land to the true faith, he hears how Dyaclisian is persecuting the Christians and goes straight to him and reproves him. In the verse *Legend of St George*[10] of the monk John Lydgate

(1370–1449), St George undertakes many journeys in his defence of the Church and the rights of widows and virginity, and on one of these adventures meets the dragon (Stanza 6). Lydgate tells the story of the passion second, linking it with the dragon-slaying with the words 'This same time . . . ' (Cf. 'At this time' in *The Golden Legend*. Caxton is more explicit: 'Now it happened that in the time of Diocletian and Maximian . . . ')

Alexander Barclay's *Life of St George*[11] is dated 1515. It is dedicated to Thomas, second Duke of Norfolk, who had been elevated to the Garter under Richard III. Barclay is an interesting character: he was first a priest in Devon, then a Benedictine monk at Ely, a Franciscan at Canterbury, and finally rector of a City of London church. Among other things he translated the Roman historian Sallust. Barclay's *Life* is an expanded verse translation of the Latin hexameter poem *Georgius* (1507 or earlier) of Johannes Baptista Spagnolo, a Carmelite of Mantua, and a very popular humanist writer, who became General of his Order in 1513. The verse mini-epic of 'the Mantuan' (as Spagnolo was called), which is pedestrian and lacking in originality but never less than 'correct', is close to the versions of Voragine and Caxton. Where there is a difference, it is usually due to the writer's humanistic leanings. His conclave of gods and goddesses, representing the forces of evil, recalls the beginnings of *Odyssey* Book V, or *Paradise Lost*, and is pure invention. As would be expected of a Latin humanist poet, there are hosts of allusions to classical mythology. Barclay, composing in rime royal (ABABBCC), translates where it suits him, and omits where he thinks it proper, so adapting his original for an English audience. He adds among other things an invocation to the Virgin, an exhortation to the youth of England, and a concluding prayer to George. His version runs to 2,716 verses, as compared with the 997 of the Latin.

In a Prologue the poet invokes the aid of God the Father, and the Blessed Virgin Mary, calling George her 'servant' and 'knight'. In setting the scene he tells us that George's 'contrey natyf' was 'Capadoce', which is 'adjacent unto the see' (but here he mistranslates the Latin *ponto*, which means not 'the sea' but the

45

province of Pontus, north-west of Cappadocia). George was born of wealthy parents in the city of Caesarea, and was converted to Christ before becoming skilled at every sort of martial prowess and achieving promotion to the rank of tribune. The poet remarks on George's extreme physical perfection and beauty, but stresses that, like Joseph and Hippolytus, he was by nature *chaste* (365ff.).

Next comes the dragon-episode, which is datable, as it takes place when Maximian (286–305 and 306–308) sends an expedition to Libya. George is in command of a legion of Thracians, which arrives at Sylena, once ruled by Duke Bacchus and home of the Sileni, his people, who have been driven from their Grecian homeland. Sylena is terrorized by 'one great dragon odyous', a *female*. 'Hyr wombe infectyf invenymyd the grounde' (542). Two citizens each day are chosen by lot to be fed to her, one at morn and one at evening. (Curiously enough, the woodcut which appears at the beginning of Barclay's poem and also before Chapter IX shows the princess with a lamb, and illustrates not his version but that given in *The Golden Legend*.) To begin with the lot fell conveniently on 'the lowest people', but finally it falls on the king's daughter, 'a fayre yonge virgyne and goodly damoysell' (595). Now the king is old and all his other children have died, so he is heartbroken. But St George is not far away when he hears of these events, and he sets out with a small company.

The king and queen try to console their daughter with promises that they will all be honoured as gods in days to come, and encourage her to fix her mind upon eternity, not 'this faynt lyfe caduke and temporall'. The daughter, now named as Alcyone, is led out 'in weddynge ornament' and chained to a pillar, and the poet is inspired to give her a lengthy lament (778–819), as the citizens watch from the walls and weep.

George crosses himself, charges and spears the dragon in the mouth, then lays about him with his sword until it shatters. With a second spear (an invention of Barclay's) he strikes through the beast's throat and heart and bursts its bowels asunder. The dragon is killed outright (as in the Latin original, but not in *The Golden Legend* or any other version we have considered) and the king and queen, overcome with joy, forget their age and run to the walls. 'All laudyd the knyghtes myght and audacyte / prayeing theyr goddes his honour to auaunce / for his preseruyng of chaste virginite' (961–3). The queen bids the hero welcome (974–87) and George addresses the citizens (1016–78) adjuring them to believe in Christ. Both of these speeches are inventions by Barclay, designed to avoid a passage in the Latin which teems with classical parallels.

After the king and queen and their daughter are christened and their idols destroyed, George teaches them all the festivals of the Christian year. The dragoness is burnt, and the scene of the conflict is recorded in paintings on the city walls and gate. Annual plays (surely an allusion to the mummers' plays of Barclay's time) are to be introduced and performed in perpetual commemoration of the event.

Now the king offers George his daughter in marriage, and promises him his kingdom as the marriage portion. (This turn of events is unique to Barclay.) But George declines. He replies: 'My mynde disposyd is nat to maryage / But from all lust to kepe my body fre' (1200). He builds a church at Sylena to Our Lady, and a healing spring wells up there. At this point Barclay omits some 'fabulous stuff' in the Latin, and substitutes an extended exhortation by the saint to the nobles and people of Sylena, in which among many other things he advises them to 'avoyde vyle venus and lustes corporall' and promotes the cause of 'abstynence'.

George now departs through Egypt for Syria and there crushes a revolt against Rome in Palestine, does some sight-seeing, visits all the Christian monuments, and learns much from the Carmelite monks there (who did not arrive in fact until the twelfth century). He then goes to Persia, where he renounces his military life for a life of sanctity.

It is here that the 'damned spirits' conspire to stir up the pagans to persecute the Christians. (In the Latin, the Roman gods sit in council in Babylon, and Minerva delivers a long set speech.) Now the passion and martyrdom of George begins: George is tortured cruelly by Dacian and healed by an angel; the sorcerer Thamyr is

47

defeated and converted. George pretends to agree to offer sacrifice, but instead smashes the idols and amid earthquake and fire from heaven many people are killed.

The king of the city (as opposed to Dacian) wants revenge, but his queen, who has secretly been converted by George, blames him for his persecution of the Christians.[12] The king is furious, and has her stripped, hung from a tree and scourged. George assures her as she expires that she will receive baptism in her own blood.

Now George is warned by angels of his impending death, and the astronomical information given ('now was clere phebus entred in the bull') dates the martyrdom to some time around 21 April. George is sentenced to be drawn through the city by bulls until torn apart, and then (rather superfluously) to be beheaded. His last prayer is that all who invoke his name will be heard, and a voice from heaven assures him that this boon will be granted. After his beheading, the tyrant Dacian, returning home, is burnt to cinders with all his entourage, and together they plummet to hell.

In the differences between the Latin of Spagnolo and Barclay's Englishing of it, we see the differences of agenda. The Mantuan, with his holy-humanist leanings, has his queen heading, not for heaven, but for Olympus, and the saints in heaven are pictured eating ambrosia and quaffing nectar. God is Jove and thunders in heaven. Barclay, by introducing the theme of chastity and renunciation, has added a significant new direction to the familiar legend. In the typical schema, a hero rescues a damsel from a dragon and he marries her. Barclay revives the convention only to break with it: our hero (who was curiously also seen from antiquity as a symbol of fertility) prefers to remain chaste, and his building of a church to Our Lady confirms his adherence to this ideal. He is Our Lady's knight. George overcomes the female dragon (symbolizing sex) and with it overcomes his own fleshly temptations.

The cult of the Virgin grew increasingly in the Middle Ages, and her association with George is illustrated by, among other things, the many dedications of churches to the Virgin and St George.

From *The Golden Legend* onwards the grateful king builds a church to the Virgin and St George (in the *Southern English Legendary*, uniquely, it is to Christ and St George); in Barclay it is to Our Lady alone. St George's chastity is Barclay's contribution to the legend. The strong connection in medieval thought between sexuality and religiosity goes back to pre-Christian, Hellenistic times. Lust became a metaphor for worldliness and impurity. Great male saints show great moral strength against the temptations of the flesh, and in the hagiographies women (other than mothers or sisters) are 'tools of Satan', and exist only to seduce the saint from the path of virtue. Man first fell through woman's weakness: Eve, the serpent and the Fall are inextricably associated in patristic misogyny. Just as 'a second Adam to the fight and to the rescue came', saving mankind from the ruin brought on him by the first Adam, so a second Eve, the Virgin Mary, who is the antitype of Eve, in the Apocalypse crushes the serpent beneath her feet and redresses the balance, achieving a perfect symmetry. Most of the major saints were virgin, and a recent study has demonstrated that those saints who preserved their virginity (as opposed to those who merely achieved continence) enjoyed a greater reputation for their holiness, powers of intercession, and miracles. Virginity is magic.[13]

This association of St George with the Virgin (the Queen of Heaven and her Virgin Knight) can also be seen in the fact that in some versions of the story it is she who heals the wounds of the tortured saint. There are visual depictions of her actually resurrecting St George from the dead, and arming him for the fight. In fact, a resurrection scene occurs in all four of the major English cycles of St George: in the chancel windows of St George's Church at Stamford in Lincolnshire (known to us through seventeenth-century sketches); in the north window of the west aisle of St Neot's Church at St Neot in Cornwall; and in the two English alabaster retables at Borbjerg in Jutland, and La Selle in Normandy.[14] Though these cycles are fairly close in date (mid fifteenth century to early sixteenth century) they differ widely in individual iconography and in choice of subject. But their most important common feature is the role of the Virgin Mary.

In this connection, we might consider briefly the sex of the dragon. Latin nouns are assigned a gender, masculine, feminine or neuter: the word for 'table', as it happens, is feminine, and 'bridge' is masculine. (In English we would of course refer to a table or bridge as 'it'.) The word used in the Latin text of *The Golden Legend* is masculine, *draco* (but presumably it could also have been feminine, or the species would have died out), and in all the English Lives the monster is referred to as 'him'. The Mantuan uses a variety of terms: *monstrum* (neuter), *bellua* (feminine) and *serpens* ('creeping thing'), a noun which is mostly masculine in poetry and ecclesiastical Latin. Barclay, however, consistently refers to the dragon as 'her'. This is clearly pointed, and the reason is not hard to discern. The female dragon is Lust, St George overcomes it with his lance, and the virgin leads it into the city, tamed by the symbol of her chastity. Samantha Riches[15] believes that in late medieval times the dragon was increasingly thought of, and depicted, as female. In the many images reproduced in her book, however, it seems unclear whether the orifice shown beneath the dragon's tail is an anus, female genitals, or even a wound made by St George's spear. In some of these pictures, where a broken, phallic lance points towards a gaping orifice, the sexual imagery is unmistakable. One need not labour the point. But if the reader thinks this interpretation far-fetched, why in almost all versions (Barclay, surprisingly, fails to seize his opportunity) does the virgin, at George's invitation, lead the wounded dragon into the city by her girdle? And why, in modern colloquial parlance, is the term 'dragon' applied only to formidable females, and never to males?

We have already scanned the Lives of St George over some 1,000 years. But there is further to go.

Not only is there a tradition that St George came to England: some sources actually seek to connect him with the origins of Christianity in this country. John Hardynge in 1543 wrote in his *Chronicle* that Joseph of Arimathea (who was supposed to be a kinsman of St George) converted a King Aviragus to Christianity and gave him the silver-white shield with a cross on it which became a 'common syne' for English armies (in effect giving him the banner of St George some three centuries before George was born). The same Hardynge relates that King Arthur (whose name was inevitably linked with that of George) used the same banner in his struggle against the Saxon foe.

Edmund Spenser, in Book I of his epic *The Faerie Queene* (the first books were published in 1590), relates how the Red Crosse Knight (the Anglican Church) protects the virgin Una (True Religion) against the trickery of the enchanter Archimago (Hypocrisy) and Duessa (Falsehood, especially that of the Roman Catholic Church). There are many reminiscences of the George-legend, including a terrifying dragon that has ravaged Una's father's realm, and Arthur, too, puts in an appearance, wearing a dragon helmet. The Red Crosse Knight is exhorted by Contemplation to abandon earthly conquest and his career of bloodshed, and is assured of a blessed end in the heavenly Jerusalem. 'For thou, emongst those Saints whom thou doest see, / Shalt be a Saint, and thine owne nations frend / And Patrone: thou Saint George shalt called bee, / Saint George of mery England, the signe of victoree.'[16] A few stanzas later we are given the original of this name. George is of the blood of Saxon kings. The faerie who stole him at birth hid him in the furrow of a field, and a ploughman found him and called him Georgos, 'tiller of the field'. George's fight with the dragon lasts three days. After the first day George is refreshed at the Well of Life; after the second he shelters beneath the Tree of Life; and on the third he runs his weapon through the dragon's mouth and slays him. Interestingly, though Una is betrothed to him, the Red Crosse Knight leaves her in order to fulfil a promise he has made to serve the Faerie Queene (Glory in general, Elizabeth I in particular, and presumably by extension also the Virgin Mary) for six years.

In Richard Johnson's splendidly entitled *The Most Famous History of the Seven Champions of Christendom* (*c*.1597), George is actually an Englishman and is born in Coventry. His romance with the Princess Sabra, the Sultan of Egypt's daughter, is straight from the pages of the swashbuckling romances of bygone days. This time George does marry the virgin he rescues from the dragon, and has three sons by her. (So much for George as an icon of chastity. But we are now in the Counter Reformation, of course, and attitudes towards family and fatherhood have undergone a sea-change.) But the princess is killed in a riding accident and the widowed hero dies killing yet another dragon, illustrating the dangers of hubris. And in this version (surprise!) there is no tyrant, no torture, and not a single mention of martyrdom. Johnson aimed simply at telling a good tale. He had no more scruples about importing details from other legends than had the earliest hagiographers. In fact his plot is based largely on *Bevis of Hampton*, a blood-and-thunder verse romance of the late thirteenth/early fourteenth century (itself based on a twelfth-century Anglo-Norman romance). Sabres rattle, blood curdles and withers are wrung. Bevis converts and weds the daughter of the King of Arabia and kills the Emperor of Germany, who had killed his father. His sword (like St George's) is called 'Morglay', and his steed, engagingly, 'Arundel'.

The legend of St George and the dragon is referred to explicitly only once in Shakespeare. This occurs in *King John* (Act 2 sc. 1). 'St George that swinged the dragon, and ever since / sits on his horseback at mine hostess' door / teach us some fence [defence]!' But he is named in oaths, his feast day is mentioned, and above all his name is used in battle cries: 'God and St George!' However, in *Richard III* Act V sc. 3, King Richard refers to the story in a desperate prayer at Bosworth Field: 'Our ancient word of courage, fair St George, / inspire us with the spleen of fiery dragons!' But the most celebrated passage of all is in *Henry V* Act III sc. 1, where the king finishes a stirring speech to his men at the siege of Harfleur (just before Agincourt) with the spine-tingling war-cry: 'Cry God for Harry! England! and Saint George! (The English archers were to be the heroes of the day, and George was, among other things, patron saint of bowmen.) The film of *Henry V*, in which Sir Laurence Olivier performed so unforgettably, came out in 1944 as timely propaganda for our forces fighting for the liberation of France. Shakespeare, who more than any other Englishman expressed with eloquence and passion the spirit and tradition of England (read the famous speech of John of Gaunt in

Richard II with dry eyes if you can), is said to have been born and to have died on 23 April, St George's Day.

But perhaps the greatest work to draw on the story of George and the dragon after Spenser was *Pilgrim's Progress* (Part I of which was published in 1678), the allegorical masterpiece of the Protestant writer John Bunyan. On his way from the House Beautiful to the Celestial City, Christian must pass through the Valley of Humiliation where he meets and fights the hideous, dragon-like beast Apollyon ('destroyer', one of Satan's fallen companions).

They meet and first engage in a bout of verbal sparring (as George does with that other fiend Dacian) in which Apollyon seeks to seduce Christian from the faith. But Christian defeats him with one argument after another.

'How many servants of Christ have been put to shameful deaths,' sneers Apollyon, 'whereas how many times have I, by power or fraud, delivered those that served me?'

'His forbearing at present to deliver them,' counters Christian magnificently, 'is on purpose to try their love, whether they will cleave to him to the end . . . For, for present deliverance, they do not much expect it; for they stay for their glory; and then they shall have it, when their Prince comes in his, and the glory of the angels.'

The combat is terrible. Apollyon 'spake like a dragon', and sighs and groans burst from Christian's heart. He is wounded all over, he falters and is thrown to the ground, his sword flying from his grasp. Desperately he recovers it, and when he is on the point of being crushed to death, he strikes at Apollyon and wounds him, and the monster spreads his wings and vanishes.

Johnson's romanticized legend of George in his *Seven Champions of Christendom* spawned a whole host of seventeenth-century ballads, two of which are preserved in Bishop Thomas Percy's *Reliques of Ancient English Poetry* (1765). In one of these, 'The Birth of St George',[17] George's mother, wife of Lord Albert of Coventry, has dreamt that she will give birth to a dragon, and, of course, George is the dragon and will be a terror to all his foes. She dies in childbirth, and George is spirited away by the weird lady of the woods, but not before Lord Albert's nursemaids have seen three marks upon his body: 'A blood red cross was on his arm / A dragon on his breast: / A little garter all of gold / was round his leg exprest.' Poor Lord Albert pines away, while his infant son is trained 'in feates of armes, / And every martial play.'

In another ballad, 'St George and the Dragon',[18] the dragon is an Egyptian variety, and is pacified with a diet of virgins. King Ptolemy's daughter Sabra, clothed all in white, is tied to a stake and preparing to be eaten when George rides up and swears by the cross upon his breast to break his lance upon the dragon's chest. He throws the beast to the ground mightily and thrusts his lance into its mouth (for he could pierce no other place), so killing him. Sabra falls for her dashing knight, but their love is not universally approved and George is dispatched to Persia where he is imprisoned. He escapes, kills a giant, and returns to wage relentless war on the heathen, sparing only Egypt. Finally King Ptolemy yields: George weds Sabra and sets course with her for home, not yet having consummated his marriage. En route, two lions kill Sabra's eunuch, but lie quietly by her side without doing her harm (so proving her virginity). Reassured thereby that his bride's honour is intact, George takes her back to England, where 'they many years of joy did see / And lived their lives in Coventry'.

NOTES

1 See Chapter 2 n. 9.
2 Revelation 12.9.
3 Or could the tradition that sets the story of George in Nobatia provide a clue? We read in Gibbon that when the Blemmyes, who lived scattered between Merowe and the Red Sea, began to trouble the Roman province of Upper Egypt, Diocletian removed the Nobatae from their settlements in the Libyan deserts to territory above Syene, above the Nile cataracts, so that they could guard the frontiers of the Empire. Could Syene perhaps have been the city plagued by the dragon?
4 Published by the Scottish Texts Society, 1891, pp. 176–203.
5 E. Mâle, trans. Dora Nussey, *The Gothic Image*, pp. 288f.
6 Lecture VII, *Lectures on the History of the Eastern Church*, as reported in R. J. E. Tiddy, *The Mummers' Play*.
7 Published in *Modern Language Notes* 38, 1923, pp. 97–101.

8   Published in *Early English Text Society* (EETS) Original Series 200, 1936, pp. 129–33.
9   Published in *EETS* Extra Series 96, 1905, pp. 132–5.
10   Published in *EETS* Extra Series 107, 1910 and 1962, pp. 145–54.
11   Published in *EETS* Original Series 230, 1955.
12   Like Pilate's wife: Matthew 27.19.
13   Donald Weinstein and Rudolph M. Bell, *Saints and Society*, pp. 73–99.
14   Samantha Riches, *St George: Hero, Martyr and Myth*, Chapter 3, pp. 68–100.
15   Riches, *St George*, pp. 156ff.
16   Book I, Canto X, lxi.
17   Series the Third, Book III, no. 1.
18   Series the Third, Book III, no. 2.

5

CHANGING TIMES

Though dismissed early on as apocryphal and suppressed by the Church, the legend of St George never lost its grip. St George became the great saint of the Crusades. With the failure of the Crusades the idea of chivalry itself began to fail and the concept of knighthood was increasingly seen as outdated. Later, in its attack on the Roman Catholic Church the Reformation condemned belief in the intercession of saints, and St George's popularity again suffered.

He always had his critics. Erasmus was among the earliest and most vehement of these. On Henry VIII's accession in 1509 he visited England and there, at the suggestion of Thomas More, composed *The Praise of Folly* (1509) in which he satirized theologians and prelates of the Church, and poured scorn on the cult of the saints and the veneration of their relics. 'The Christians now have their gigantic St George,' he commented, 'as well as the pagans had their Hercules.'

But St George had become part of the fabric of England's history, and this was largely because he had been adopted by the English monarchy as their particular patron. It had begun with Richard the Lionheart, who is said to have seen a vision of St George at the siege of Acre in 1191, and was continued by his great-nephew Edward I (1272–1307) who chose to fly St George's banner beside those of England's two other patron saints, St Edmund and St Edward the Confessor. But it was under Edward III (1327–77) that the monarchy's special devotion to St George reached its zenith, and this is evidenced at the outset of his reign by the so-called 'Milemete

Treatise' (1326–7), a document which offers advice to the young king on his duties as monarch: it bears an illustration in which St George himself, wearing a tabard and epaulettes with the distinctive red cross, presents the new king with a shield displaying the three lions passant guardant which are his royal arms. Further evidence of this association was shown in some wall paintings (now lost) in the Palace of Westminster, in which the saint leads Edward and other members of his family towards the high altar. He had made a practice of rewarding his soldiers with gifts of images of the saint, and is said to have invoked the saint's aid at the successful siege of Calais in 1349. Edward's throne was embellished with a carving of St George and the dragon, and it is known that he possessed a reliquary supposed to contain some of the saint's blood.

But Edward III's devotion to St George is demonstrated above all by his institution of the Most Noble Order of the Garter (c.1348) and his establishment of the focal point of the Order at St George's Chapel at Windsor, a building which is crammed with visual imagery referring to St George. Once, too, there was a statue of George and the dragon there; a painting of St George with Edward the Confessor on the rood screen; and a reliquary with three of his bones. The king was lavish in his generosity to the chapel: when he commissioned an alabaster reredos for the high altar it took ten carts each drawn by eight horses to convey it from Nottingham to Windsor.

This was devotion indeed, and it was the Order of the Garter, more than anything else, that established George as the country's sole patron saint. The chapel at Windsor had in fact been a royal chapel dedicated to St Edward the Confessor, so in rededicating this as solely 'St George's Chapel' Edward was making a significant gesture.

Officially the Order was placed under the patronage of the Holy Trinity, the Virgin Mary, St Edward the Confessor and St George (in that order) but very soon the last named became first in importance. From its beginning the Order was elitist and limited to the richest and most powerful in the land: its purpose may have been a specific one – to inspire England with fresh zeal for recovering the Holy Land; or perhaps it was aimed more generally at uniting the nobility behind the king (his father, Edward II, had been deposed in sordid circumstances) and providing a focal point for loyalty to the English cause.

At its foundation, the Order consisted of the king and his son the Black Prince, each at the head of a cadre of 12 knights. This is the highest order of knighthood in Great Britain, and still thrives today, with the reigning monarch and Prince of Wales at its head, and 24 other worthies and 26 knights (or Ladies Companion). The Order is still required to assemble on the eve of St George's feast day at Windsor, wearing the coveted 'Greater George' (a collar with the gold Badge Appendant, which is a richly enamelled image of St George slaying the dragon), and the 'Lesser George' (another representation of the dragon-slaying) worn attached to the Sash.

The Order became at once a symbol of loyalty to England and its crowned head, and its patron saint's close association with the English cause and with English pageantry was thus sealed for all time. France had St Denis: England had St George. And soon after Edward's momentous gesture there was the first official celebration of the saint's feast day. However gorgeous the pageantry that took place on 23 April 1349, however splendid the masses celebrated in thanksgiving, we know that the Grand Feast enjoyed by the Order on that first St George's Day celebration was rich by any standard.

> *First Course*: Sallet, Loin of Veal larded, Green geese, Carpes, Haggest Pudding, Chickens boyled, Turkey pye, Salmon, Piggs, Chine beef, Gammon Bacon and Pullets, Pidgeons, Chicken Pye, Wild Boar Pye, Baetilia Pye, Venison Pye, Shoulder Mutton in blood with Steakes, Capons, Kid, Veal.
>
> *Second Course*: Sallet, Gammons, Bacon, Ducklings, oysters, Sweet-bread, tame Pidgeons, Rabits, Peacock Pye, Dried Tongues, Sparagrass, butter'd Crabs, Lamprey Pye, Jelly, Blamange, Tarts, Anchovis, Caveare, and Pickled oysters.

The identification of St George with 'Englishness' is further illustrated by the Wilton Diptych (gloriously displayed in the National Gallery) which was painted in the 1390s for the private devotions of Richard II. On the right panel we see the Virgin and baby Christ with angels, and one of the angels carries a staff with a red cross banner, underscoring the association of St George (England) with the Virgin. Recent cleaning has also revealed details which suggest that Richard is depicted symbolically offering England to the Virgin as her dowry.

If Edward III's reign represents the apogee of the cult of St George, his successors to a greater or lesser degree maintained the tradition. Henry V (1413–22) was devoted to the saint. On embarking for France in 1415 he ordered his people to pray to St George for his safety, and when, after five weeks, he had taken Harfleur, he flew the banner of St George alongside his royal standards over the city, and decreed that the cross of St George be worn by all English troops. The saint was seen over the battlefield of Agincourt in 1415 (where 1,500 English beat 50,000 French) and in the wake of this massive victory Archbishop Chichele elevated George's feast day to the status of a 'duplex maior', a 'greater double festival' (which made it the equal of Easter Day or Christmas Day, or the feast of an Apostle), and it became a national holiday on which everyone could be freed from work and go to church.

An illustration in the famous Bedford Hours (1423) shows John, Duke of Bedford, kneeling before St George, who wears the sovereign's robes of the Order of the Garter. John was Henry V's most trusted brother, and had been left to rule the country when Henry set off for France in 1415. In this illustration we can see the interconnectedness between political, religious and national symbolism. George here represents the English nation. When Henry VI was crowned in 1429, aged eight, there was a mime, or tableau vivant, of St George at his coronation feast. On one side of St George (England, Henry's inheritance) stood the Virgin Mary (England was called 'the Virgin's Dowry') and St Denis (France, which was also part of Henry's inheritance).

By this time St George had become recognized as the patron of English royalty and the English nation, and reverence towards him had become part of the duty of the monarch. Edward IV (1461–70 and 1471–83) was to exploit this link in order to legitimize his claim to the throne. The white roses of York are scattered all over the chapel at Windsor, which he began to rebuild in 1475. And other monarchs were to manipulate this association for their own ends: after the Battle of Bosworth brought the Wars of the Roses to an end in 1485, among the standards presented by Henry VII at St Paul's was one of St George; and there was once an altarpiece in the Royal College at Windsor depicting Henry VII's family kneeling in prayer beneath a splendid version of the battle between George and a flying dragon. Henry had part of a leg of St George, and in his will bequeathed a gold statue of the saint for the high altar at Windsor. His tomb, too, is embellished with yet another 'George and the dragon' scene. Henry VIII (1509–47) had an image of St George on one of his crowns and on suits of armour; in 1526 he minted gold nobles with the 'George' and the dragon' scene on them, the first to appear in England.

During all the soul-searching that went on during the Reformation the saint's fortunes were bound to fluctuate. Yet when Henry VIII in 1536 banned almost all religious feast days, he excepted those of the Apostles, the Virgin Mary, and St George. Not long after this, however, in 1552, the Bishop of London banned the observance of St George's Day.

The humanist critics certainly provoked a great deal of healthy scepticism. In the fourth year of his reign, the 13-year-old Edward VI (in a story related by John Foxe, the martyrologist) was able to ask members of his court: 'My Lords, I pray you, what saint is St George that we here so honour him?' The Marquess of Winchester replied: 'If it please your Majestie, I did never reade in any historie of St George, but only in *Legenda Aurea [The Golden Legend]*, where it is thus set downe, that St George out with his sword and ran the dragon through with his speare.' The young Edward was speechless with mirth, but asked at length 'I pray you, my Lord, and what did he with his sword the while?' In a very careful, and perhaps uneasy reply, the Marquess said: 'That I cannot tell your Majestie.' It was a pointed question. Within a couple of years the second Book of Common Prayer was to abolish all saints' days.

But St George survived.

It was the special devotion to St George on the part of the monarchy that sealed his connection with nobility and authority. Originally, as a warrior saint, he had appealed to a nation constantly at war; as a martyred Christian he appealed to a Christian nation fighting for the cause of Christendom; as a knight and patron saint of the Crusades, he no doubt appealed strongly to the English knightly class. Caxton tells us: 'This blessed and holy martyr St George is patron of this realm of England and the cry of men of war.' According to Froissart he was invoked by English troops at the sea battle of Sluys in 1340, at Crécy in 1346, and at Poitiers in 1356. But his appeal was more general and went deeper. He was patron saint of soldiers and sailors, of horsemen and archers and armourers and ironworkers and saddlers and butchers; of barren women and expectant mothers and indeed of all mothers. Because of the assumed etymology of his name, he is also patron of farmers and labourers and protector of crops and animals, especially horses, cattle and sheep, and their guardian against wolves. He was invoked as a protection against plague, syphilis and leprosy, and temptation, madness and witchcraft. His powers as intercessor in time of trouble were second to none. In England, as elsewhere in Europe, George had become popular with the hoi polloi. He had been transfigured by the passage of time into much more than a warrior saint and martyr and a model of knightly chivalry. He had acquired a large variety of meanings and different spheres of importance in our national life. And precisely because he was neither martyred nor buried in England, shrines were erected to him all over the country; because he lacked connections to specific places or groups of people, he became a symbol for all England.

The story of his death and renewal, with its universal resonance, mirroring the passion of Jesus himself, may even account for the placing of his feast day near Easter, with its theme of resurgence and resurrection coinciding with even older agricultural celebrations. There are some 100 wall paintings of him in churches in this country: in Norfolk alone he is featured on seven screens; he is regularly included in Books of Hours (these were books containing prayers, psalms and other useful texts for the devotions of pious lay people, and mostly date from the late fourteenth to early sixteenth centuries). George appears in the East Anglian Book of Hours (c.1480) as one of a group of martyrs who might be invoked in time of need. Indeed, George was one of the 14 Holy Helpers, a group of saints whose cult was first established in the Rhineland in the fourteenth century. These saints were regarded as especially efficacious when invoked against diseases and at the hour of death.

St George's Day traditionally marks the beginning of spring sowing. (According to the traditional French rhyme 'A la Saint-Georges / sème ton orge. / A la Saint-Marc / il est trop tard' – there is only two days' margin for error.) After prayers to St George, the cattle were garlanded with greenery and driven off to summer pasture. His link with increase, new life and fertility is deeply rooted and ineradicable. Associated as he is with greenery and foliage, fresh garlands and branches, he is inevitably confused with other such figures, such as 'the Green One' of Islam (Al Khidr); the Green George of the Black Forest; our own Jack-in-the Green (who takes part in May Day revels covered with boughs and leaves, and by wearing the livery of the 'god' is ensured of his protection); and the Green Man (a fertility symbol based both on legends of St George and on pagan myths) who is married to the Queen of the May after she is brought in procession to the churchyard.

St George became the patron of country spring and summer festivals, and a stock figure in the miracle plays which were performed at the start of spring on his feast day, or on May Day – that day so redolent of the death of the old and the birth of the new. In these plays the story of St George and the dragon was acted out in towns and villages all over the country (e.g. at Lydd and New Romney in Kent, and Plymouth in Devon).

One of the ways in which St George was firmly entrenched in the popular imagination was his appearance in the fifteenth and sixteenth centuries in parades called 'ridings', in which an actor played the role of St George and there was a model dragon. Anthropologically speaking, the ridings which took place on St George's Day (some on Midsummer Day) are classed as 'lustrations', rituals in which (at least originally) 'the fertilisation spirit was borne in solemn procession from house to house and round all the boundaries of the village'.[1] The same thing can be observed in Catholic countries today when the effigy of the patron saint is carried around the village boundaries (the *festa* is a rallying point and a communal reaffirmation of membership to a community, a total fusion of the religious and the secular). These ridings may originally have been folk memories of the pre-Christian walks around the fields in springtime, but in medieval times they had become an excuse for a municipal celebration. From the fourteenth century, they were organized and provided for by a guild, and we have a good deal of detailed information about what went on in the records of the Norwich Guild of St George. The Norwich riding was already a fixture by 1408.

The guilds were a very prominent feature of late medieval life, but Guilds of St George were specially prestigious. Membership was in theory open to all, but in practice the Guilds of St George tended to include most of the most powerful members of the community. Guilds were socio-religious organizations, and members (who paid a fee: Saxon *guildan* means 'to pay') enjoyed privileges and incurred certain obligations. Nominally members met to observe their patron's feast day together, provided support for any of their number who needed alms, and had masses said for departed guildsmen. There were many Guilds of St George elsewhere in cities such as Chichester, Coventry, Reading, Leicester, Exeter and in towns as small as Woodbridge and New Romney. They were hierarchical and, though ostensibly religious in purpose, they became in practice powerful political blocs. It was almost obligatory for anyone who had political ambitions to become a freeman of the guild. This was true of other guilds, too, but especially true of the Guild of St George, which in several towns became the *de facto* governing body.

In Chichester, Sussex, for example, there was an extremely ancient guild, which was possibly in existence in pre-Norman days. After a period of decline, it was confirmed by Royal Patent of Henry VI as the Guild of St George, and had an image of the saint in the cathedral (images of St George are common in and around Chichester). Like other guilds the Chichester Guild was allowed to hold lands in order to finance the daily services in its chapel, where prayers were offered daily for the king. The members of the guild were the most influential and respectable citizens, and its Master was the Mayor of Chichester. The importance of being a freeman of the guild may be seen in the fact that this was one of the three requirements for the right to vote for the MPs of Chichester.

The Norwich Guild (about which we know a good deal) had its own altar to St George in the cathedral, its own priest who said mass there daily, and a special St George's bell, which was tolled when the guild attended church. One can imagine the awe inspired in the common people by the sight of the guild, passing with all its wealth and in all its pomp and splendour, in solemn procession towards the cathedral. It was a show of authority and power which could not fail to leave its mark.

In the ridings provided by the Norwich Guild, 'the George', a man in armour and gorgeously decorated gown, accompanied by a club bearer, henchmen, banner carriers, musicians, torch bearers and holy-water carriers, went in splendidly colourful procession with the dragon, the guild priest, and the whole court of the guild and freemen of the guild in capes and gowns of red and white. The procession began at the church of St Peter Mancroft, and was led by a man carrying a gilded wooden sword with a dragon-head hilt, which Henry V was said to have presented to the guild when granting its charter in 1417. It passed to a wood outside the city, where the battle between St George and the dragon was re-enacted. Such at least was the original scheme: in the sixteenth century, George was assisted by another character, 'the Margaret', who presumably played the role of the rescued princess (though her name recalls another saint credited with the killing of a dragon). The dragon, known later as 'the Snap' or 'old Snap', was made of wickerwork and painted cloth or of iron and wooden hoops, had flappable wings and a movable head, and was manoeuvred by a man concealed within its body. After the fight the procession returned to the cathedral, a solemn mass in honour of St George, the king and the guild was celebrated (for all except the dragon, who was shut outside) and a splendid feast was held. Then there were more prayers in the cathedral. Next day a requiem mass for the founder, benefactors and the souls of departed guildsmen was celebrated, after which the annual elections for guild officials were held.

These colourful and splendid occasions were an excellent opportunity for the guilds to display their wealth, civic power and munificence. At Norwich St George's Day was the focal point of the whole year. We know most about Norwich, but there were ridings elsewhere too; they are recorded in large cities like Leicester, Coventry, Stratford, Chester, York and Dublin; but also at humbler locations such as Lostwithiel in Cornwall, where the local guild laid on an annual procession, with a member playing the part of St George, and this was followed by the Office of the Dead, a feast, and on the next day a requiem mass. At Reading, Aston and Louth, for example, a figure on horseback known as a 'George' stood on a 'loft' in the church, so no doubt these places staged their own ridings.

In some places, the feast of St George's Day was celebrated with the performance of a miracle play. There was a St George play in Lydd, Kent, in the fifteenth century, and probably also in New Romney nearby, and one is recorded (on St Margaret's Day) in the sixteenth century at Bassingbourn, Cambs. These were apparently real dramas. Their subject was the legend of St George, of course, but sometimes this was combined with a treatment of the legend of St Margaret, a figure with whom he is regularly associated.

In 1547 Edward VI prohibited all processions, associated as they were with disorder, and the Chantries Act of the same year, which ordered the dissolution of all England's intercessory institutions, should have done away with all the religious guilds at a stroke. But the guilds generally survived and the festivities continued, even if in slightly altered form. In the mid sixteenth century the court of the Guild of St George at Norwich felt moved to opt for a procession without George or Margaret, but still felt the need for the traditional dragon. In fact, the Norwich dragon survived until the dissolution of the guild itself in 1732.

Guilds will have fared differently in different areas. In Coventry, for example, the festivities of 23 April ceased, the guild broke up, and the local chapel to St George was abandoned. But the guild at Norwich, protected by Henry V's charter, continued, though in reorganized form, as the 'Company and Fellowship of St George' – a title reflecting the new rejection of the doctrine of purgatory which underlay the foundation of these religious fraternities. Catholic features of the annual celebrations were removed: prayers for the deceased were discontinued; religious services no longer honoured St George exclusively. What remained had a much more Protestant flavour: evensong on the eve of the feast, divine service and a feast on the day itself; and on the following day a sermon and elections.

Our knowledge of guilds elsewhere is scant, but in York, for example, the Guild of St George and St Christopher was dissolved in 1547 after the Act of Parliament banning guilds and processions; however, the festivities of St George's Day were reintroduced only seven years later. Processions were, after all, one of the expressions of medieval communal religion, and they were not going to die out overnight.

Under Queen Mary the customary Catholic ceremonies were restored. The guild at Chester, for example, restored its processions and gifts of alms to prisoners. In 1555 Norwich decided to revive its earlier celebrations, but the procession now took place on the Sunday after Trinity, and inevitably lacked something of its former glory. The celebration never reverted to 23 April, and other changes simply underlined the break with the old religion, until finally the St George celebrations became merged with other days important to the local calendar. The restoration to Catholicism

66

was short-lived. The foundations of the older traditional practices had been undermined for ever, and the changes to the St George's Day celebrations mark a significant new phase in the relationship of religious and political life in the city. What had once been a demonstration of piety had now become merely a symbolic way of bowing to the establishment.

With the accession of Elizabeth, Protestantism was revived: St George's feast day at first received official sanction by its inclusion in the 1559 Prayer Book. But only a couple of years later it was removed.

There had been a huge transformation in these annual celebrations. Soon more or less all that remained was the dragon. In the early seventeenth century a 'fool' was included in proceedings, to detach the festivities even further from their original significance. In Chester in 1610 the traditional event was replaced by a horse race: true, St George rode in the procession, but at his tail, almost inevitably, came the Mayor and his corporation.

St George may also have been seen in morris dances at Maytime (in the unlikely company of Robin Hood and Maid Marion and the clown, the fool and a hobby horse) because on occasion a dragon made an appearance, and it is thought that George may actually have ridden it. Sword dances, which are closely related to morris dances, were rituals performed at particular seasons of the year as part of agricultural festivals, and designed to preserve the ordered sequence of the seasons and to ensure the fertility of the earth. In the celebrated sword dance of Papa Stour (one of the Shetland Isles) there are seven dancers, each representing one of the Seven Champions of Christendom: St George himself, St James of Spain, St Denis of France, St David of Wales, St Patrick of Ireland, St Anthony of Italy and St Andrew of Scotland.[2] Unlike the morris dance, which is simply a dance, the sword dance is always dramatic in form. Its meaning is variously interpreted, but the connection with sacrifice seems well established. And the mumming play (in which the dance element has been relegated to the background, if it has not disappeared entirely), found in various forms all over Europe, is clearly an allegorical presentation of the death of the old year and the birth of the new. It always involves a fight, a death and a renewal – the symbolic victory of light over darkness, or warmth over the cold.

Our evidence for the mumming play (which evolved from the sword dance) is late and dates mostly from the nineteenth century, but clearly these plays owe their origins to much earlier times. Texts in loosely rhyming verse exist from all over England, Wales and Ireland (in Scotland another hero takes the place of George), and there are countless local variations. The plays were performed generally in mid-winter, but on May Day at Manchester and in Norfolk on Plough Monday in early spring. St George was not originally a part of these plays, but was imported at some later stage (as was Oliver Cromwell later still). He was after all a very suitable candidate, being in origin, at least, a hero of death and revival.

The play's principal characters are St George (or Sir, or King, or Prince George), a Turkish Knight, Captain Slasher, and the Doctor. A supporting cast of minor roles would vary considerably in different versions: at Newbold near Rugby the characters were: Father Christmas, Moll Finney (mother of the Turkish Knight!), Humpty Jack, Beelzebub and 'Big-Head-and-Little-Wit' (the last three of which appeared only in an Epilogue, while Beelzebub goes round taking a collection).

There is a Prologue, and the two combatants introduce themselves. St George challenges the Turkish Knight, they meet in battle and one or other of them is killed. (In the Newbold version it is the Turk's turn, in the Lutterworth play it is St George's.) Enter the Doctor, who, after fulsomely advertising his medical expertise in lines interspersed with gibberish, revives the dead man.

Thomas Hardy introduces a mumming play in *The Return of the Native*, and has his heroine Eustacia Vye disguise herself as the Turkish Knight so that she can meet Clym Yeobright, with whom she is infatuated. Hardy paints a hilarious picture of an extremely amateurish effort, with thumbnail sketches of the characters, including Father Christmas, swinging a huge club, and the Leech, with his bottle of physic slung under his arm. In Hardy's play, a

Valiant Soldier (Slasher) challenges the Turk in George's name. When the soldier is slain St George enters with a flourish:

> Here come I, St George, the valiant man
> With naked sword and spear in hand,
> Who fought the dragon and brought him to the slaughter
> And by this won fair Sabra, the King of Egypt's daughter;
> What mortal man would dare to stand
> Before me with my sword in hand?

A fight ensues. Eustacia, as the Turk, sinks to the floor slain (but manages to die against the clock-case so that her head is in a position to view proceedings). One can well imagine the fun of such productions. 'For mummers and mumming Eustacia had the greatest contempt,' Hardy wrote sympathetically. He surely speaks from first-hand experience: like Eustacia, he had suffered.

The minor characters display a bewildering variety of names, Captain Slasher (Beau Slasher, Bold Slasher, Captain Bluster) seems of quite uncertain provenance and is not always distinct from the Turkish Knight. A mixture of Saints and Kings, Dukes and Lords support St George, Slasher and the Turk in minor capacities.

The Doctor is an amusing character and offers some scope for a talented actor. The speech in which he boasts of his skills is a set-piece. 'What can you cure?' asks the King of England in the Lutterworth version. The Doctor seizes his cue:

> All sorts of diseases
> Whatever you pleases:
> I can cure the itch, the pitch,
> The phthisic, the palsy and the gout;
> And if the devil's in the man,
> I can fetch him out.
> My wisdom lies in my wig,
> I torture not my patients with excations [sic]
> Such as pills, boluses, solutions and embrocations;
> But by the word of command
> I can make this mighty prince to stand.

The foregoing is sufficient to give the reader a taste of the unique flavour of the demonstration.

The dragon is rarely involved, but in the Brill version he plays a prominent role, and is attacked by the whole company together. In a Cornish version, where St George fights the dragon, the Princess Sabra appears in a mute role. One is irresistibly reminded of amateur pantomime in a small seaside town.

The play is to do with fight and resurrection, and the two main roles are the combatants. The minor characters are variations of the 'grotesques' that grace nearly all the village festivals, characters that owe their origins to magical or sacrificial custom.[3] Though of no relevance to the plot, they are as essential to the mummers' play as principal boys and dames are to pantomime: they are a survival, and though they may have some tiny part in the drama, they are generally brought on to be seen only after the duel and before the collection.

In the St George Play performed in some of the villages near Lutterworth in Leicestershire at Christmas 1863 (its text was published in 1865) the Prologue is spoken by Slasher; Prince George is the King of England's son, no less, and wears a sword, and the Turkish Champion carries both sword and pistol. Other characters are a Noble Doctor, Beelzebub and a Clown. Prince George is laid low, and the Noble Doctor revives him (for ten pounds). Enter Beelzebub with club and frying pan (this is for the collection) and the Clown ('My head is great, my wit is small, / I'll do my best to please you all'). The whole company sings a song of farewell: 'And now we are done and must be gone, / No longer will we stay here; / But if you please, before we go, / We'll taste your Christmas beer.' And in some 90 lines all is done. *Exeunt Omnes.* Enough!

The hero has ensured that winter is once again banished and that spring can return. As in the old spring rituals, when the old and the new king fought (to the death, originally), a death is followed by a rebirth. George, whose name in its Greek form means 'tiller of the soil', 'worker of the earth' (as does the name of the Persian god Mithra), was inevitably connected with agriculture, with the sowing of seed, and with rebirth. In some versions of his life he is killed and resurrected no fewer than three times. And since the Church has always tended to absorb the village agricultural celebrations into the various festivals in its calendar, how, with all his resonant associations with pre-Christian traditions, with his many-layered legend and its theme of death and renewal, could St George fail to find an enduring place in the hearts and minds of the people of England? He was everywhere: on wall and screen and altar in church, in mad plays, in gaudy pageants and processions, in folk ritual, on the farmland, in the guildhall, and on the village green.

So by hook or by crook he survived. But as we have seen, he survived in a somewhat altered form, and his survival should not be taken as a reflection of the survival of traditional religious feeling. In fact, as one writer has argued, the persistence of St George represented practically everything except the continuity of tradition.[4]

The real saint had become sidelined, his commemoration secularized. The establishment had claimed him for its own purposes.

NOTES

1 E. K. Chambers, *The Mediaeval Stage*, vol. 1, p. 118.
2 Jessie L. Weston, *From Ritual to Romance*, London, Anchor Books, 1957, p. 94.
3 Chambers, *The Mediaeval Stage*, vol. 1, p. 214.
4 Muriel McClendon, 'A Moveable Feast: Saint George's Day Celebrations and Religious Change in Early Modern England'.

6

SURVIVAL IN THE MODERN ERA

The tomb of St George can be seen today at Lod (Lydda) about 15 miles south-east of Joppa. It belongs partly to Muslims and partly to Greek Orthodox Christians. Lydda was a town, but because of its frontier position enjoyed the importance of a city. At some stage, possibly as early as the time of Hadrian (though the earliest coins found belong to the time of Septimius Severus, c.202 AD) it was given the new name of Diospolis. There was a bishop of Diospolis in the fourth century, and a Synod was held there in the fifth century. Lydda held the saint's relics, his tomb was in the town, and pilgrims visited it regularly. A church stood there from at least the sixth century, possibly even earlier; tradition has it that it was built by St George's uncle or brother, and subsequently rebuilt by Constantine the Great. In the seventh century the church and tomb were demolished by Persians. It was rebuilt, ruined again on the approach of the First Crusade, then rebuilt by the Crusaders. On the approach of Richard the Lionheart, Saladin destroyed it again, and tradition has it that Richard contributed to its reconstruction. Again it was rebuilt in the twelfth century, and again destroyed, yet again rebuilt and yet again destroyed. In the nineteenth century a Greek Orthodox church was built over the scant remains. Apparently the town was commonly referred to by its hero's name, rather than as Diospolis or Lydda, and might still have been so called had it not been for a long break in Christian pilgrimage there from the sixteenth to the eighteenth centuries.

George had his critics, but his roots went deep and the people do not so lightly abandon their heroes. In their histories Sir Walter

Raleigh (?1554–1618) and Peter Heylyn (1600–62) defended his historical authenticity; Sir Thomas Browne in his *Pseudodoxia Epidemica* (1646) was of the same opinion. Gibbon's disingenuous identification of the martyr with the heretical Arian George was utterly refuted by the Catholic apologist John Milner in 1795, whose conclusions were confirmed at the turn of the twentieth century by the Jesuit scholar Hippolyte Delehaye. The findings of historians and archaeologists have increasingly tended to corroborate the view that George was a real martyr, that he died around the end of the third century AD, and that his cultus was established very soon after his death.

In England the Reformation took its toll, but there was always resistance to it. The foundations of traditional religion having been undermined, the tradition itself was reinvented: George survived because he changed. The high-water mark of the monarchy's devotion to St George had come with the Tudors. Later rulers showed less enthusiasm for maintaining this connection, but equally they were ready to exploit it to their own advantage. Charles I, at least, seems to have been a great admirer of the Order of the Garter and its code of chivalrous behaviour. The Rubens portrait of St George in *St George and the Dragon*[1] painted for Charles I in 1629–30 is too like the monarch for this to be anything but an allegorical celebration of Charles's triumph over evil (he had overcome the threat of war with France and Spain), and the princess he rescues is clearly his queen, Henrietta Maria.

In the later Stuart period Charles II, James II and Queen Anne all chose St George's Day for their coronations. The link with the saint had by now become a traditional means of bolstering the prestige of the monarchy.

During the backlash to the Reformation, St George enjoyed a revival with the discovery of Africa, India and the Americas. The Church sent missionaries everywhere, and everywhere they took with them the archetypal legend of the Monster-Slayer, the hero who confronted evil and triumphed in the name of the Church. When the Portuguese missionaries introduced him in Brazil,

George was identified by the natives with Ogun the forest hunter. George was endlessly adaptable.

And wherever the British went, churches, towns, schools, hospitals and hotels were named after St George (or one or other of the Hanoverian monarchs called George). The name had become our hallmark. A glance at the index of any atlas will reveal a mass of such dedications in the 'new countries', in New York, New South Wales, Quebec, Guyana, Delaware, Virginia, Cayman Isles, Malaya, Prince Edward Island, Queensland, Ontario, New Brunswick, Newfoundland, Bermuda. There are Georgetowns in Guyana and Malaysia and South Africa. (Georgia (USA) is named after George II, whereas the Republic of Georgia is named after its own indigenous people, the Gukz, but the country came to be associated with St George, its patron saint.) In the later eighteenth and nineteenth centuries, cathedrals were dedicated to St George at Kingston (Ontario), Madras, Kingston (St Vincent and the Grenadines), Freetown (Sierra Leone), Cape Town (South Africa), Perth (Western Australia), Wellington (New Zealand), Georgetown (Guyana) and Jerusalem. And today there are Anglican churches of St George in Andorra, Belgium, France, Germany, Italy, Norway, Portugal and Spain.

When mass marketing was ushered in by the Industrial Revolution, the image of St George became synonymous with good craftsmanship and honest value. The St George mark meant 'made in England' (or Britain), with the implication that it was therefore the best of its kind. The name or symbol of St George was promoted as proof of English quality, and often the words 'British Made' can be seen on products made actually in England, illustrating how until recently 'English' and 'British' were often more or less interchangeable terms. Manufacturers chose 'St George' as the brandname for all sorts of products, considered by them to be standards of excellence – for a type-face, for example, for chess sets, for a series of books on classic English writers.

'The George and Dragon' is of course a favourite name for public houses (five are listed in my local Yellow Pages, plus three George Inns and four George Hotels); as is 'The Lamb and Flag' (originally 'The Holy Lamb and Flag' in which the lamb is the sacrificial Lamb of God, and the banner, a long, flowing white flag with a red cross, is the banner of the Resurrection, derived from the vision of Constantine the Great and the attribute of warrior saints Ansanus and George, Reparata, Ursula and the Phrygian Sibyl).

The Christian name George, incidentally, though it was always popular in the East (as Yuri, Georgi, and Yegor in Russia, Gheorghe in Romania, and Georgios in Greece), more or less came over to England with George I. There is scarcely a single 'George' listed in parish registers before 1700, though subsequently it became, together with John and Charles, the most common of Christian names. Edward III, who was so zealous in his attachment to St George, called not one of his seven sons George: for the name to appear in his family we have to wait until George Duke of Clarence, his great-great-grandson, was born in 1449. The name had been used, it is true, by a few families, like the Nevilles and the Villiers, in the fifteenth and sixteenth centuries, but otherwise it is rare until the advent of the House of Hanover. Thereafter, there was an unbroken succession of King Georges for 116 years.

St George and the dragon first appeared on English coins in 1526, in the reign of Henry VIII. Then, for the first time since the Middle Ages, they reappeared on gold coins in the reign of George III, in 1817, when the Italian émigré Benedetto Pistrucci's classic design, with the surrounding legend 'Honi soit qui mal y pense', won a competition held by the Prince Regent. Since then the familiar image has regularly appeared: it was used by Queen Victoria in e.g. 1884 and 1887, and in the last century it appeared on gold sovereigns in 1958. Most recently St George has been featured on millennium issues.

St George is also remembered in the chivalric orders founded under his patronage. The Order of the Garter is the most famous, but there are many others. The Constantinian Angelic Knights of St George is supposed to be the earliest of such orders and tradition claims that its foundation, by Constantine himself, was as early as 312, coinciding with his celebrated vision of the Cross on the eve of the Battle of the Milvian Bridge. In fact, probably the earliest of the monarchical orders of chivalry, though it was much shorter lived, was the Order of Saint George founded in 1325 by Charles I of Hungary, slightly predating the more famous Order of the Garter. A similar order was founded in Aragon in 1371, though it too was short lived. Many such orders foundered as time went by, through political upheaval or too close an adherence to the original founder.

In the eighteenth century, Orders of St George were established in Bavaria and Russia, but increasingly the trend was towards democratization. However, in the nineteenth century and since, most governments in the West have felt it incumbent upon them to maintain these orders, or at least to pay them lip service if not actively to foster them, and the tradition spread in the twentieth century even to communist countries as well.

The founder of the Constantinian Order of St George, which still exists, was according to tradition Isaac II Angelus Comnenus, the twelfth-century Byzantine emperor. In the fifteenth century the brotherhood was active in fighting the Turks in the Balkans, and in the sixteenth century the family claiming descent from Isaac was recognized by the Papacy as true heirs to the throne of Constantinople. At the same time their military brotherhood was recognized. The aim of the Order, which in practice has tended to be restricted to old, aristocratic Roman Catholic families, is the propagation of the Catholic faith. Though it still has among its members many aristocrats (especially of the Two Sicilies) today there are also scholars and industrialists to leaven the lump.

In England in 1818 a second Order of Chivalry was established by the Prince Regent, later George IV, the Most Distinguished Order of St Michael and St George. The aim of this new Order was to reward diplomatic services, and membership was originally limited to inhabitants of the isles of Ionia and Malta and the Britons who had served them there. (Later, in 1879, its scope was widened to include anyone, British or foreign, who had done exemplary work in the Commonwealth.) This Order was subsequently reorganized (by William IV) to embrace three classes of

Knights, in descending order of importance: Knight Grand Cross (GCMG), Knight Commander (KCMG) and Companion (CMG). George IV (who chose to celebrate his official birthday on his name-saint's feast day, 23 April) was anxious to win popularity, both on his own account, and also to make up for the failures and mistakes of his father George III. The medal of this new Order has St George and the dragon on one side, and on the other St Michael and the devil, and bears the portentous legend: '*auspicium melioris aevi*' ('augury of a better age'). In the event George IV failed to gain for the monarchy the respect the Hanoverians had so far lost (this was left to Queen Victoria and her consort); but his Order has always enjoyed the highest prestige, and once again renewed and confirmed the English tradition of St George as the symbol *par excellence* of patriotism and loyalty.

Our saint was adopted by other institutions, too, like the utopian Guild (or Company) of St George, founded in 1871 by the painter, writer and social campaigner John Ruskin. This was a society he founded to enact his economic doctrines, and above all to combat the inhumanity and avarice of uncontrolled industrial development. The aims of the Guild were basically philanthropic and patriotic: Ruskin wanted to establish the dignity of agriculture, to teach the skills of husbandry in special schools, to house labourers decently, and to buy up land for cultivation. He was passionate in his desire for social reform to alleviate poverty and combat the evils of industrial society. St George would have appealed strongly to Ruskin, with his deeply patriotic and pro-imperial feelings.

Then there was the Royal Society of St George, founded in 1894 and still, like Ruskin's Guild, very much in existence. Its aim was to promote everything that encouraged patriotism and pride in England and its heritage. The Society has its own charter, granted by Elizabeth II in 1963. 'Even today,' its prospectus trumpets, 'though some of the old glories and certainties may have dimmed, England still maintains her inner strength, her quiet dignity. No longer the hub of a great empire, but still the bastion of freedom, gentility and human decency – values which give meaning to the clarion cry "St George for England".'

Before the American War of Independence, Societies of St George existed in the Colonies for the support of British immigrants. Subsequently they spread all over North America. During the Civil War many loyalists crossed to Canada and founded societies there. Today there are 76 branches throughout the world, with a membership of over 10,000. Flowers are sent to the Queen on her birthday; on St George's Day a ceremony is held at the Cenotaph, and a service of thanksgiving is held on the Sunday nearest to 23 April. 'Englishness means fair play, good manners, chivalry,' the prospectus continues. 'In earlier times it was a byword for integrity and honesty.' Just so.

In 1908 St George was chosen as patron saint of the Boy Scout movement. For its founder Baden-Powell, the chivalric code with its emphasis on honour and loyalty, on courage, discipline and a sense of fair play, seemed the perfect ideal to which the youth of England should aspire. Lieutenant-General Robert S. S. Baden-Powell was a cavalry officer, who distinguished himself in the relief of Mafeking, and in 1908 he wrote *Scouting for Boys*, in which he described the games and competitions he had devised to train his cavalry troops in scouting. His book became very popular and a new movement was born. By 1910 Sweden, Mexico, Argentina, the United States of America, Canada, Australia and South Africa had their own Scout troops, and by the late twentieth century there were Scouts in 100 nations. His idea was to develop boys aged 11–15 in the values of good citizenship, chivalry and a variety of skills in outdoor activities. Scouts were expected to show loyalty to their country, to help others, and to obey the simple code of chivalrous behaviour which formed the Scout Law. In 1910 Baden-Powell answered the demand for a girls' equivalent of the Scouts by founding the Girl Guides, and in 1916 a movement of younger boys called the Wolf Cubs was begun. The Girl Guides similarly established their own junior group called Brownies, for those of seven years and upwards, and embraced similar ideals: a code of behaviour, devotion to community service, and the development of skills in various useful activities.

On St George's Day each year Scouts must remember the Scout Promise and the Scout Law, and there are Scout and Guide parades up and down the country which culminate in a service at the local church. In his *Scouting for Boys* Baden-Powell relates (mistakenly) that the knights of Arthur's Round Table chose St George as their patron 'because he was the only one of all the saints who was a horseman', and he was the patron saint of cavalry, from which the word 'chivalry' is derived. (Once again, George is linked with Arthur. In 1929 a curious, anonymous work called *St George at Glastonbury* tells of a Cornish-born George who travels to Glastonbury, becomes a knight and is given the sword Excalibur, which two centuries later was to be carried by Arthur, then later by Richard I.) Baden-Powell was fascinated by the idea of the knight errant, fearless and decent, courteous and pure, going about doing a good turn every day, and his choice of St George was pointed. Young men should get out into the open air and build themselves decent characters by helping others.

Books more patriotic than historical appeared linking St George with Constantine the Great and with Arthur and his knights, and cartoons depicted clean-cut young Scouts with clean knees either actually spearing a dragon or rolling up their sleeves and 'being prepared'. The cover design for the 1922 edition of *Young Knights of the Empire: The Wolf Cubs' Handbook* (first published in 1916) shows a youth clad in armour, holding a fleur-de-lis shield in one hand and a banner of St George (displaying the title and author of the book) in the other, as he guards a dragon slumped behind the bars of a prison. The bars are labelled variously with logos such as 'Honour God and the king', 'Do a good turn to someone every day', and watchwords of the Scouting movement like Obedience, Thrift, etc. – implying that it is by observing these rules that the beast (sex? indolence? the foreign foe?) is kept under lock and key. The dragon seems utterly vanquished: its once fiery breath leaves its nostrils in a wisp of extinguished vapour.

The Scouts and Guides, Wolf Cubs and Brownies have until now flourished in the United Kingdom and abroad. But today there is a crisis in the movement, not apparently in recruitment of youngsters, but of adult leaders. Adults today are more wrapped up in their own pleasures and less inclined to put themselves out for other people than they were. Where once an employee's involvement with a youth group brought his employer's commendation and active encouragement, it is now taken as evidence of his lack of commitment to his job. There is also nowadays the unfortunate association with paedophilia. One wonders what Baden-Powell would have made of such attitudes, or indeed what he would have thought of the current Guides Association handbook, which includes a picture of a Girl Guide holding an unrolled condom in her hand (presumably as part of a sexual health campaign).

St George had been 'the crie of men of warre' since the Crusades; he had throughout English history been called on in time of trouble and appeared with banner flying to aid troops fighting in the cause of justice. Wartime tends to throw into prominence a nation's characteristics and promote its unity, and it was natural that St George, the embodiment of Englishness, should be used (both for us and against us) in wartime propaganda. During the Boer War he proved a useful symbol to those promoting the English cause and attacking the Boer dragon.

A World War I recruiting poster shows, in a roundel, an image of a stout St George, on a rearing white charger, thrusting his lance deep into the breast of a huge, threatening war-dragon. Above and below the legend reads: 'BRITAIN NEEDS YOU AT ONCE'. He also appears in a number of cartoons of the period. And once again, when they called on him (and there are several instances of British troops invoking him in their hour of peril) he answered their need. There was a celebrated sighting of St George at Vitry-le-François, where a Lancashire Fusilier saw the saint on a white charger at the head of the British troops. More than once an army of angels was seen, famously at Mons. After the war, Adrian Jones' fine Cavalry Memorial in Serpentine Road, Hyde Park (1924) depicts St George in the moment of victory over the dragon brandishing his sword triumphantly aloft.

In the 1939–45 war, perhaps because the 'war to end all wars' had left a land less than fit for heroes and disillusionment had set in, he made fewer appearances either in propaganda or on the battlefield. But, as has been mentioned earlier, the film of Shakespeare's *Henry V* (with Olivier playing the king) was used to stiffen the sinews of the British troops fighting in France, and urge them to 'imitate the action of the tiger'. 'Once more unto the breach, dear friends, once more,' cries the king, 'or close the wall up with our English dead!' (Act III sc. 1). And he rounds off his most famous speech with an electric call to arms: 'I see you stand like greyhounds in the slips, / straining upon the start. The game's afoot; / Follow your spirit; and, upon this charge, / Cry – God for Harry! England! and Saint George!'

King George VI was so deeply moved by the courage shown by his people during the Blitz, and especially in the disposal of bombs and mines, that in 1940 he introduced the George Cross, which is on a par with the Victoria Cross. The Cross is awarded for 'acts of the greatest heroism or of the most conspicuous courage in circumstances of extreme danger', and like the V.C. can be awarded posthumously. It is usually given to civilians, though it can also be won by military personnel for acts not usually attracting military decorations. The George Cross shows on one side the saint with sword drawn trampling on the dragon, and the inscription FOR GALLANTRY: on the other side is the name of the holder and the date. The whole island of Malta was awarded the George Cross in April 1942 for its heroic resistance. The George Medal, introduced for acts of outstanding bravery (but of lesser magnitude), is a silver disc bearing on one side the image of the monarch, and on the other St George and the dragon.

St George's cult is so intertwined with English history, our traditions and popular culture, that scenes from the saint's life have always been a stimulus to the artistic imagination. We have seen something of what survived the stripping of the altars during the Reformation, in the late 1540s and 1550s, when most of the old rood screens and altarpieces were demolished, and the iconoclasm of the Commonwealth accounted for much more. In one day alone, on 20 January 1644, a joyful thug called 'Slasher' records in his diary that he 'did' eleven churches near Ipswich. He charged 6s 8d per church, and in a period of 50 days he visited more than 150 churches, smashing windows, fonts, statues, and taking pot shots with his pistol at saints and angels too high for him to reach with a sledgehammer. So much has been lost; yet so much still remains, and some at least of what was left has now passed to the safety of galleries and museums.

In the late eighteenth century, St George began to appear on Staffordshire pottery and on prints as a hallmark of patriotism. And in the so-called Gothic revival of Victorian times he is seen on prints and on book plates, as well as in the paintings of the Pre-Raphaelite Group. A series of paintings on the life of St George was executed by Sir Edward Burne-Jones (1833–98), who, with the rest of his circle, was fascinated by knights and ladies and the ideals of chivalry. Dante Gabriel Rossetti in 1857 painted a splendidly romantic watercolour of *The Marriage of St George and Princess Sabra*, based on the later romanticized version of the legend.[2] The two lovers huddle in a close embrace, and in the background angels supply them with the music of bells, which they strike with tiny hammers. The dragon's head, still grotesque in death, pokes from a box in the foreground. In a homely touch, the princess, in order to submit to her lover's embraces, has hung her crown from a hook on the wooden panelling.

The V & A possesses another treatment of the wedding of St George and the princess, a glass panel executed by William Morris and Dante Gabriel Rossetti as part of a cycle of the saint's life. We are shown a rather anxious George clasping the hand of a swooning princess, a careworn king with his sceptre and orb, and his queen, who supports her daughter and peers nervously down from a balcony. Below, two heralds blow their trumpets, as the dragon's severed head is displayed on a trencher with the sword that brought him low. These sentimental, pseudo-medieval representations of post-medieval legend present a striking contrast with the earlier paintings of St George by Uccello (*c.*1396–1475), Crivelli (active 1457–93), Pisanello (mid-1400s) and Tintoretto

(1518–94) in the National Gallery, London. In Renaissance versions of the fight with the dragon, the princess is nearly always shown on her knees in prayer, or running away in fright: Tintoretto has chosen to show her dropping to the ground as she flees. In the clouds above, some heavenly presence is shown coming to St George's aid. Interestingly, the dragon's last human victim is intact (one normally sees bits and pieces) and disposed in an attitude clearly intended to evoke that of the crucified Christ. In the bottom right painting of the predella of Crivelli's *Madonna della Rondine* we see St George astride a stallion, his sword raised to strike a dragon who has a broken lance piercing his throat. Behind, in the far background, the princess kneels in prayer, and the king and queen watch from the balcony of the castle gatehouse.

In Uccello's painting there is also a cloud-whorl suggesting heavenly intervention. The princess, strangely, holds in her hand the girdle to put round the dragon's neck, but it is evidently a spare girdle, for she is wearing another. St George also appears in the same gallery in two other paintings, one by Giorgione (d.1510) and the other attributed to Palma Vecchio (d.1528).

The western medieval images of St George are to a greater or lesser extent idealized, but they belong to a world we recognize, and if it is not an everyday world, it is one that creates natural effects and relates to the external world we perceive with our senses. In the East we sense a quite different order of things. It is, in fact, another world. Take for example the fifteenth-century icon of St George and the dragon of the Novgorod School in the Russian Museum at Leningrad. There is a total absence of violence: instead we are shown a stillness illustrating the calm after a spiritual struggle has been won. The faces of both George and the speared dragon display an unearthly calm; not the slightest hatred or fear is expressed. The icon is the image of the inner life. The artist has depicted a spiritual combat, and the look on the saint's face is one of radiance and inner joy.[3]

Composers, too, have found inspiration in St George as a figure of patriotic Englishness. The prolific Sir Arthur Sullivan

(1842–1900) used some of the music he had written for his first ballet *L'Ile Enchantée* (1863) in his *Thespis* (now lost) (1864), where it appeared in part of the ballet entitled 'St George and the Dragon'. This same music he used yet again in the 'Friar Tuck and the Dragon' scenes of his 1897 *Victoria and Merrie England*, written to celebrate Queen Victoria's diamond jubilee. Sir Edward Elgar (1857–1934), the composer most closely associated with stirring, patriotic music, set two libretti about St George. At the age of 39 he composed a cantata for chorus and orchestra called 'The Banner of St George', and in 1911, to mark the inauguration of New Delhi as India's new capital, he composed the music for Henry Hamilton's *Imperial Masque*.

Edward German's Arcadian *Merrie England* (1902), an unjustly neglected work, was hugely successful in his day, as were his three dances for Shakespeare's *Henry VIII*, which were household favourites. 'Long live Elizabeth!' cry the Chorus, 'Sing with united breath, God save Elizabeth and England, Merrie England! May Heaven prosper her, May heaven foster her, Saint George for Merrie England, and England's Queen Bess!' And if the message has yet to sink home, later on we are given an 'Egyptian Dance' – a Masque of St George and the Dragon.

And no attempt, however skimped, to follow our saint from his arrival in England to the present day can afford to overlook Mrs Clifford Mill's children's play *Where the Rainbow Ends*. Premiered in 1911, this play is now largely forgotten, but in its day it was so popular that it became an annual Christmas treat until the 1950s, rivalling even Barrie's *Peter Pan*. It still crops up as an end-of-term play in the more traditional prep schools. A hundred years on it is not easy to enjoy the smug chauvinism, but children loved it from the start and no doubt their parents thoroughly approved of its message.

The plot concerns two children, Crispian and Rosamund Carey. After their parents are lost at sea they live with a hard-hearted uncle and aunt, who turn the parental home into a hotel and plan to sell their father's library to a German-Jewish business-man called Schnapps. This is simply too much.

With two school chums and their baby lion 'Cubs' they set off in search of their parents to a never-never land where all lost loved ones are found. When they summon St George, he is a disappointment: he is weaponless, humbly clad and suffering from neglect at the hands of the English. But Rosamund insists that she is a damsel in distress and needs his aid, and flash! he is transformed into a hero in dazzling armour, complete with sword and cloak. They leave together on Faith's magic carpet, hotly pursued by evil uncle and aunt and the loathsome bellboy, who has summoned the Dragon King himself.

When the advance party reaches St George's Territory they are safe, but it is deep in the Dragon King's country, and around them the darkly looming Dragon Wood threatens. The children wander into the forest and are captured by the Dragon King who sentences them to be thrown from the castle ramparts. In the nick of time the two boys climb the tower of the castle, take down the dragon flag and run up the banner of St George. In a twinkling, St George himself appears, fights the Dragon King and kills him. Enter Rainbow Children singing triumphantly. The play ends Where the Rainbow Ends and all lost loved ones are found, as the Carey parents, who have been castaways nearby, are reunited with their children. Together they go back home to good old England, taking St George back where he belongs, once and for all.

In an Epilogue St George makes sure that the audience have not missed the point: 'But, you know, all of you will have Dragon Woods to go through at some time in your life . . . '. Asking them to promise to be on the side of St George against the Dragon King, he concludes: 'Rise, youth of England, let your voices ring / For God, for Britain and for Britain's king.' And all rise and sing the National Anthem. Curtain.

Nothing is easier than to mock the cherished ideals of the past, but there is an earnest self-righteousness and smug insularity about the work which jangles horribly. One notes that in the revised version published in the 1950s the German Jew Schnapps has become a ludicrous Frenchman, M. Bertrand (who seems to have wandered from the set of some TV farce), and St George's final couplet is turned into something of rather broader appeal: 'You of all nations, pledge yourselves to fight / For peace, for Justice, Freedom and the Right!'

If our saint is invoked today, he is usually a caricature of himself for he crops up coxing and boxing with John Bull and Britannia as an emblem of all that is fine (and ridiculous) in our country. By turns St George either spears iniquity or is seen to be tilting at windmills.

Or else he is invoked by dangerous right-wing causes masquerading as 'patriotic associations', whose uncompromising message is the superiority of Englishness and the evil influence of non-English stock. One such organization is The League of St George, founded in 1975, whose members insist on the exclusive innate right of the true-born English to call themselves English, and talk of the necessity of expelling foreigners in order to preserve the pure blood of the 'Folk'. These institutions give patriotism a bad name.

If for centuries our patron saint was invoked in war, today he is increasingly a presence in sport, which is after all a sort of ritualized warfare. England's sport, in the last quarter of the twentieth century, has suffered a terrible decline. In 1989 our soccer team was placed eleventh in FIFA rankings. In 1999 in the Wisden World Test Match ratings our cricket team was placed ninth in the league of nine, and in the football World Cup we were knocked out of the first round, in the company of Kenya and Bangladesh. Fortunately things seem to be improving. There are signs that the English malaise, at least in the major sports, is being checked.

When England won the football World Cup in 1966 Wembley was awash with Union Flags: yet the Union Flag was never the flag of England. Gradually the truth has dawned: 'British' and 'English' are not interchangeable terms; the United Kingdom is not a nation state and never was (and it is not united). The charismatic John Bull figure, who with his Union Flag and red-white-and-blue waistcoat loyally supported England for so long, has disappeared for ever. Increasingly at international matches English soccer, rugby and cricket fans are waving the banner of St George and painting their faces red and white.

The Scots insist on their national identity, and in their desire to assert it they have adopted as their national anthem a song whose words and music were written as recently as 1969.[4] Its words tell of a glorious past and a glorious, resurgent future. The Welsh sing 'Land of my Fathers' with Celtic passion and tunefulness. They know who they are. The Irish, too, in 'Amhran na bhFiann' declare their undying loyalty, singing that they are soldiers whose lives are pledged to Ireland. Fine, stirring stuff. And what do we English sing to cheer our rugby heroes to victory? A lugubrious spiritual, 'Swing Low', whose tune goes nowhere and which inevitably peters out because no one knows the words. The BBC has chosen as its theme music for England's rugby internationals Holst's 'I Vow to Thee, My Country' (a 'hymn' poached from his *Planets* suite) – a fine tune, no doubt, but nostalgic and dirge-like. The Women's Institute has appropriated 'Jerusalem'; 'Rule Britannia' is stirring, certainly, but with uncomfortable imperialist associations. And 'Land of Hope and Glory' seems unsuitable on similar grounds. (Other nations are arguably just 'as blest as we', we are unlikely to rise 'still more majestic', and our bounds are hardly likely to be set 'wider still and wider'.) Perhaps we must await the composition of some new song that will manage to be rousing without being triumphalist, and which will sum up our present and future aspirations without belittling our achievements of the past. It is a tough order.

NOTES

1   The Royal Gallery, Buckingham Palace.
2   Tate Britain, London.
3   On the interpretation of icons, see R. Temple, *Icons and the Mystical Origins of Christianity*, Shaftesbury, Element, 1992.
4   'Flower of Scotland', composed in the mid 1960s by Roy Williamson, who died in 1990.

AFTERWORD

Our saint has travelled far – from his martyrdom in the Near East across the seas to England; from the time when his was a name honoured by monks but unknown to the English people, to his establishment as patron saint of England, patron of the Order of the Garter, and symbol of English patriotism and martial prowess; through his suppression during the Reformation and his subsequent re-invention and survival, by hook or by crook, through many dynastic upheavals, to the end of the second millennium, and beyond. His short life seems very short indeed when compared with his 1,700 years of afterlife.

On the east wall of my parish church there is a series of tabernacles housing paintings of the Apostles and saints. And there he is, our saint, instantly recognizable, in the furthest niche on the lower left. But is this the swarthy, pain-ravaged Turkish martyr who was torn and broken on the wheel? It is not. This George is beardless, youthful and beautiful, and stands, with hips tilted slightly, in a languid Pre-Raphaelite pose, behind a king-sized shield. (It is a sentimental version of the famous Donatello statue created for the church of Orsanmichele in Florence. But there the master has given us, along with physical grace, virility, and along with youthful vulnerability, dignity and defiance.) Could this be the war hero who was boiled alive and who speared the fearsome dragon? Alas, like Bottom, he has been translated. This St George is absolutely at home in the land of warm beer and cucumber sandwiches.

His history has not been uneventful.

In 1222 (perhaps a little later) a church Synod decreed that his feast day should be kept as a holiday of the lesser rank. In 1399 it seems to have become an officially recognized national holiday, and in 1416 it was established as one of the principal feasts of the Christian year. By this time George was accepted as the special protector of England; he was the country's most venerated saint; he represented King and Country, and his eastern provenance was either forgotten or ignored. In the First Book of Common Prayer his feast was printed in red letter; but in the revised version of 1552 it was moved to 21 April to make way for St Mark the Evangelist, and demoted to black-letter status. In 1553 Catholic Mary restored the ancient services with the traditional Latin liturgy of the Roman Church. Then in 1559 Protestant Elizabeth (for various reasons, none of them religious) restored its red-letter status and returned it to its proper day. Under James I it reverted again to a black-letter day, this time permanently. There was no return to the Catholic invocation of saints, and in the Church of England 23 April was no longer celebrated as a solemnity but only as an optional feast day. (A comparison of pre- and post-Reformation prayers to the saint makes the point: while the former allude constantly to the saint's intercessory powers, the latter ask for 'a courage like that of St George' to cast aside earthly honours and as 'soldiers of Christ' to seek only to please him.) The propers were abandoned, and the ordinary lessons and psalms for that time of year were read.

During the seventeenth and eighteenth centuries (until 1778) for all Catholics 23 April was a holy day of obligation. But in 1960 the feast was removed from the Calendar of Saints by the Sacred Congregation of Rites, and in 1969, as the result of further revision, St George's Day in the universal Roman Calendar became an optional *memoria* (an optional observance for local celebration only). However, provision was made for its observance in England, and Wales, as a *festum*, a major feast. The 1980 Anglican Alternative Service Book gave common lessons and psalms for all saints who were martyrs, like St George. Yet in 1997, interestingly, the General Synod of the Church of England restored his feast day in the new Anglican Calendar as a major religious holiday. The propers are triumphantly appropriate: the first reading (1 Maccabees 2.59–64) refers to Hananiah, Azariah and Mishael and 'the fiery furnace' and talks of the strength that comes from trust in God; in the Epistle (2 Timothy 2.3–13) Paul urges Timothy to 'endure hardships as a good soldier of Christ'; and in the Gospel (John 15.18–21) Jesus warns his disciples to expect persecution.

Sic transit gloria sancti.

In these pages we have concentrated largely on the medieval period when devotion to the saint was at its most intense. Much that has been described is lost for ever and will not return. What made us what we were is no longer in place to make us what we are. Many of the ideals symbolized by St George are outmoded: they suited our imperial past, some would say, and they have served their purposes.

Today, while Scottish, Welsh and Irish nationalism flourishes, English nationalism is for some reason not quite proper. Meanwhile, one by one, our English traditions and institutions are being eroded. A small library of 'Whither England?' books has been occasioned by the new millennium, some of them uttering gloomy prophecies of imminent doom, others rapturously embracing a brave new world. Where are we going? There are those who predict a new, more parochial kind of nationalism, one based on much narrower interests, on regions, perhaps, and individual cities. Still others predict the imminent collapse of the United Kingdom and regard devolution as simply a postponement of its final demise. Change seems inevitable.

Is it possible that St George will play a part in this brave new world? We English do not have the patriotic literature we might have. We possess the tales of Arthur, of course, but he was a Celt, and only adopted by us in the Middle Ages. We also have old poems about foreign heroes such as Beowulf, but nothing that tells of the glorious deeds of the Anglo-Saxons in their desperate attempts to repel stream after stream of invaders. This gap has meant that for many people English history begins with the

Normans.[1] Yet the Normans systematically and ruthlessly trampled on a culture that was already rich and ancient. They destroyed our books, they determinedly obliterated our history. And to our rescue, into this monumental vacuum, rode St George.

St George encapsulated the glory of the past. Add to this the significance of the dragon he slew, a symbol carried by the dreaded Roman cohorts and by our bitter foes the Welsh. ('Will the Welsh dragon devour the English!' asked one journalist on the eve of the Six Nations Rugby Championship in 2001. In the event England made a meal of it, winning 44–15.) St George was perhaps uniquely suitable to become our patron saint, to embody our heroic past and symbolize our defiant present. The implausibility of his legend and his distant origin in no way troubled the popular mind. His story was a parable of profound significance, both moral and religious. The saints are superhuman in their practice of all the virtues and their lives urge Christians to emulate them. 'Their life is a concrete realization of the spirit of the gospel, and from the very fact that it brings home to us this sublime ideal, legend, like all poetry, can claim a higher degree of truth than history itself.'[2] There are historical truths and eternal truths: legend transcends the one in order to proclaim the other.

On 1 April 1998 (a day chosen with wonderful aptness) the Foreign Secretary declared that from that day on the United Kingdom would be known as 'Cool Britannia'. But the Kingdom is increasingly disunited. In 1995 for the first time in its history a well-known greetings card manufacturer produced a St George's Day card, and by 1997 it was selling 50,000. In the opening ceremony of the Euro '96 competition at Wembley, there was a spectacular tableau of St George and the dragon. Thousands of spectators daubed red and white paint on their faces and became living banners of St George, a phenomenon which has since been noticeably on the increase. Regarded as it is by many as more 'neutral' than the Union Flag, as less aggressively reminiscent of our imperial past, it is surely our flag of the future.

The United Kingdom may be in danger of imminent dissolution. Some believe that the United Kingdom was established to serve the interests of Empire, and that with the loss of Empire it no longer has a *raison d'être*.[3] Will England in fact do better to go its own way? An England in Europe, perhaps? An English Republic even? If so, St George, though no longer invoked in pious litanies, may once again come to our rescue and real patriotism may be revived – that pride in belonging to one's country that can happily coexist with a larger view of things; a reasonable, honest patriotism that has no fear of losing itself in integration with Europe, nor, if need be, of ploughing its own course alone.

St George can once again be our inspiration. This may be the moment.

NOTES

1   For fuller argument see Rebecca Colman, 'St George for England', in *Contemporary Review* 270, April 1997, pp. 169–73.
2   Delehaye, *Legends of the Saints*, pp. 230–1.
3   Norman Davies, *The Isles: A History*, London, Papermac, 2000, p. 199.

INDEX